Dislocations:
The Selected Innc
of Paul Muldoon

DISLOCATIONS

The Selected Innovative Poems
of Paul Muldoon

selected and introduced by
John Kinsella

LIVERPOOL UNIVERSITY PRESS

First published 2020 by
Liverpool University Press
4 Cambridge Street
Liverpool
L69 7ZU

British Library Cataloguing-in-Publication data
A British Library CIP record is available

ISBN 978-1-786-94224-1 cased

Typeset by Carnegie Book Production, Lancaster
Printed and bound by CPI Group (UK) Ltd, Croydon CR0 4YY

Contents

New Poems

Acknowledgements

'The Electric Orchard', 'The Glad Eye', 'Clonfeacle', first appeared in *New Weather*; 'Lunch with Pancho Villa', 'Epona', 'Boon', first appeared in *Mules*; 'Promises, Promises', first appeared in *Why Brownlee Left*; 'Mary Farl Powers: *Pink Spotted Torso*', 'Glanders', 'From Strength to Strength', 'Yggdrasill', 'Quoof', first appeared in *Quoof*; 'Ontario', 'My Grandfather's Wake', 'Gold', 'The Mist-Net', extracts taken from '7, Middagh Street', 'Capercaillies', 'Meeting the British', first appeared in *Meeting the British*; 'Asra', 'The Panther', 'The Briefcase', extracts taken from 'Madoc: A Mystery', first appeared in *Madoc: A Mystery*; 'Incantata', 'Yarrow', first appeared in *The Annals of Chile*; 'The more I think of it', 'Not for nothing would I versify', 'Much as I'm taken', 'I look out the kitchen window', first appeared in *The Prince of the Quotidian*; 'The Mud Room', 'The Plot', 'Symposium', extracts taken from 'Sleeve Notes', 'A Journey to Cracow', 'A Half Door near Cluny', extract taken from 'Hopewell Haiku', first appeared in *Hay*; 'Hard Drive', 'Winter Wheat', 'As', first appeared in *Moy Sand and Gravel*; extracts taken from 'Horse Latitudes', 'Tithonus', 'Bob Dylan at Princeton, November 2000', 'The Outlier', 'Flags and Emblems', 'Riddle', 'The Mountain is Holding Out', 'Hedge School', first appeared in *Horse Latitudes*; 'Three Plows', 'Macgillycuddy's Reeks', 'Come Close', 'Going through the Hoops', 'My Ride's Here', first appeared in *General Admission*; 'Plan B', 'Maggot', 'The Rowboat', 'Lines for the Centenary of the Birth of Samuel Beckett', first appeared in *Maggot*; 'At The Lab', 'Federico García Lorca: "Death"', 'Seven Selfies from the Château d'If', 'The Firing Squad', 'Álvaro De Campos: "Belfast, 1922"', '*Los Dissidentes*', 'Noah & Sons', first appeared in *One Thousand Things Worth Knowing*; extract taken from *Bandanna*; extract taken from *Shining Brow*. Copyright Paul Muldoon. Reproduced by permission of Faber & Faber Ltd.

'Plan B' reproduced by kind permission of the author and Enitharmon Press, www.enitharmon.co.uk.

'The more I think of it', 'Not for nothing would I versify', 'Much as I'm taken', 'I look out the kitchen window', from *The Prince of the Quotidian*, reproduced by kind permission of the author and The Gallery Press, www.gallerypress.com.

'Hunting With Eagles, Western Mongolia, 2016', 'Walnuts', 'Zoological Positivism Blues', 'April In New Hope', 'Cuttlebone', 'Every Town It Had A Mayor', 'I Gave The Pope A Rhino', 'Likely To Go Unnoticed', 'Lonesome George', reproduced by kind permission of the author.

Many thanks to Professor John Kerrigan for reading and commenting on the introduction and afterword to the book.

John Kinsella

Introduction

This collection of Paul Muldoon's poetry is not a 'greatest hits', though many of the poems included would also fit that bill, but the collation of a body of work that emphasises and highlights the more linguistically innovative, formally adventurous, and culturally and politically challenging poems from his extensive oeuvre. Paul Muldoon constantly reminds us in these poems that he is always in some way a 'traditional poet', yet always, too, one who is at odds with tradition.

Both inside and outside the 'avant-garde', Muldoon is ultimately a maverick whose unique voice is nonetheless steeped in the politics of a bilingual Irish poetics, with a forensic dissection of 'New World'–'Old World' (false) verbal dynamics. We see and *hear* his poems in juxtaposition and proximity, in terms of those elements of his work that are possibly less appreciated and discussed by those who *might* still cast him as a lyrical *purist* who 'plays' with language. His is emphatically the voice of a poet reclaiming language (Irish, but ultimately English as well) in which the Hedge School is not of the past, but an ongoing resistance against the colonising drives of the English language. Some critics see him as more 'neutral' in terms of Northern Ireland and the Republic, but I think this challenge to separation linguistically and politically is embedded in the texts. In remaking English, Muldoon reclaims and resists.

Muldoon's poetry is compelled, propelled and 'political' in complex arrays, and is not about 'gameplay' per se, but a politics of language. Muldoon might be fixated on what language can generate in itself, but I believe he ultimately has a driving 'external' purpose in all he writes, and the reader and listener might begin to get a sense of the possibilities of this purpose in engaging with this book. Roger Rosenblatt, writing in *The New York Times Book Review*,

1

described Paul Muldoon as 'one of the great poets of the past hundred years, who can be everything in his poems – word-playful, lyrical, hilarious, melancholy. And angry. Only Yeats before him could write with such measured fury.'[1] All of this seems true to me, and to many of Muldoon's readers, but in this selection we try to delve even further into the dislocations of Muldoon's poetry through juxtaposing poems that work in quite different ways towards an impossible reconciliation of the complexities of presence and the necessities of language to explain the past and the present.

It is essential to appreciate that Paul Muldoon's journeying from his birth place in County Armagh in 1951 to his eventual life in America, especially New York, has not been a linear one, but a circuitous one. The Irish diaspora is not merely a concept; it is a gritty reality with ongoing fluxive implications for those who migrate and those who 'remain behind'. Further, there is a colonised Ireland in the north, and a decolonised Ireland of the Republic, and they are still one Ireland. The tensions of Muldoon's language evolve out of the tensions of 'The Troubles' of his youth, and the tensions and conflicts still evidenced in the 'Peace' of the present. As Muldoon's biographical note says, he is 'a former radio and television producer for the BBC in Belfast', and this connection with voicing 'home' through the machinery of the British state means the responsibilities of how language is wielded in occupied places – because for some the north is still an occupied zone, while for others it is not – and the consequences of how one makes utterances matter at a visceral street level.

This is the aspect of Muldoon's highly intellectual poetry that is often missed – it is evidenced in his songs so inspired by blues and rock. Consider his skilful use of 'plain speech', refrain, building detail, colloquial banter and intimacy, wry song-chat and (often literary) 'jokes' ... and oddities in content of seemingly 'straightforward' songs that lift them into the realm of hybrid poem-texts showing what a song lyric can do as poetry, often telling a bit of a story with asides ... one phrase tripping into another ... listing and building

---

1 https://www.nytimes.com/2016/01/10/books/review/roger-rosenblatt-by-the-book.html.

and returning – see the 'lyrics for songs' in *General Admission*, 2006. It is also shown in the conflicting voices of claim, presence, and rejection that occupied his youthful/earlier poetry. Further, though existing in a literarily attuned portion of America for many decades, and fully 'acclimatising' in terms of place, this experience of slippage between what is said and how it might be received has informed both sensitivity and bluntness to the American political landscape. It is not surprising that Muldoon, especially in his voice-play, has an uneasiness of colonial irony of presence; his engagement with his dislocations is often confronting, even abrasive, and always at the mercy of his poetry's ability to speak back with him out of its intensity of linguistic variation, slippage, fusion of root sources, and the instrument of the mouth itself. Sometimes his poems seem like actions of the mouth muscles in conversation with ideas rather than a mere device to express these ideas.

Muldoon is not categorisable; he is a prisoner of neither geography nor national identity, nor of his many influences. Which does not mean he is insensitive to political and cultural issues relating to his Irish heritage: in fact, quite the opposite. The slippage in language and identity that underlies his poetry actually brings him closer to a way of seeing these issues that is revitalising and deeply empathetic. It also allows for celebration in those odd places not normally examined. Irish poetry will always be the driver for Muldoon, we might feel sure, but American poetry, 'British poetry', diasporic poetry, embracings of and departures from Modernism, myth, tradition and reworkings of the poetry of non-English, especially Irish-language writers, not only result in interesting versions of originals, but inform his entire practice of transcribing and palimpsesting language.

Yet there's never an appropriative intent in this, though he sometimes sails close in his confronting 'enthusiasm' for engaging any 'available' or discovered language/expression/word itself; however, they are risks someone has to take in poetry in English, and he does. The question becomes whether Muldoon is trying to influence the writing of poetry, or is operating in that maverick, displaced way in which he actually overrides rather than overlays other spaces, but works off it at a tangent. I would say this is the case: I see Patrick Kavanagh's rural moments embodied in 'conventional forms' that suddenly come slant, and odd, and disorientate us, because the path of learning was fraught with obstacles and harsh realities; I see Dylan Thomas letting loose in so many drafts of a poem that they might constitute a book in themselves; I see and feel indirect influences of poets like Ted Hughes (considerable, in its own way), Federico García Lorca (New York! New York!), John Ashbery (New York! New York!), T. S. Eliot (profound connections), Ezra Pound, W. H. Auden, Emily Dickinson, the collective body of historic poetry in Irish, W. B. Yeats, of course, but equally so do I sense a 'rock' album like Lou Reed's *New York* (New York! New York! and that 'statue of bigotry') wrestling with the dislocations of migration, of marriage, of 'becoming' American as well. Then there's Robert Graves' varied and dislocated poetry of war and migration, and even (in a 'rascally way'?) Robert Graves' father ... this from Muldoon's 1998 Clarendon Lecture's volume, *To Ireland, I* (Oxford University Press, 2000), which has resonances regarding my comment a little further on about Muldoon resisting the didactic in his poetry in conjunction with issues of writing place and belonging (from near and far in Muldoon's case):

> Or the Gael in *Songs of the Gael*, a collection published in 1925 by Alfred Perceval Graves (1846–1931), father of Robert Graves. It was Graves who had asked the question, 'Has Ireland a National Poet?', alluded to by Yeats in his 1896 piece for *The Bookman*. 'We do not use the term national in the sense of belonging to the Nationalist party in Ireland,' Graves had reflected, with cunning circumspection, in his 1888 essay in *The Reflector*, 'We wished to make use of our word national, as distinguished from Nationalist, clear from the outset'. This distinction, and Graves's sense that he needs to announce it, sets up in a word or two a supreme difficulty facing the Irish writer. Can he or she adequately reflect the complexity of the Irish political situation without becoming a propagandist? (pp. 42–3)

Interestingly, in his verse libretto *Bandanna* (as with 1993's *Shining Brow*, it was written for American composer Daron Aric Hagen),

Muldoon does deploy a didactics to some extent in terms of nationalism and nation in what is seen as an 'American opera' (John Von Rhein, *Chicago Tribune*) via narration and echoes of 'popular song' (the character 'Cassidy' is 'Irish-American'). This opera deals with 'illegal immigrants' from Mexico with what might now be seen as strong anti-Wall sentiment, but also runs in tension with who can and should tell these stories, whether they are constructed or not. Muldoon has always made poetry where he feels a necessity to do so, and there's no doubt an attempt to weave a way openly through seemingly contradictory politics in this poem-song-making. There's a struggle of intent regarding labour and bigotry, and of great interest in this is where fairness is able to locate itself. Between Kane saying: 'Marx, of course, is out of favour today/because of the Commie thing' and insulting the impoverished (Kane is actually a labour organiser), we have the 'Migrant Workers' coming back with:

> For, if we organize,
> there's a chance we might yet rise
> above the harrows, the rollers,
> another day, another dolor,
> past the campfires where we cook,
> over all that's overlooked ...
> There's a chance we might steer clear
> of this endless vale of tears ...
> There's a chance we might get off the hook.

So anything we say too easily about Muldoon will likely be undone by Muldoon himself. He avoids the didactic, but can be so when 'voice' demands, and he will 'repeat' what he hears (even when 'offensive') to make a poem drive itself, but his intent is always fairness and justice entangled with an astonishment at the power of language both to damage and to heal at once. I bring this up to show that one can too easily present a 'version' of Muldoon's poetry when no single version will do. We are dealing with puns, paradoxes, and shifting meanings constantly – and if we take anything literally, we are missing the complexity of his acts of poetry. Again, as with

5

so much Muldoon, *Bandanna* (1999) is an act of collaboration – it lives with music/singing/scoring/performing – and collaboration challenges our reading of hearing of the unique in the stereotype, and vice versa; the poetry is always challenging anything we expect. In Muldoon, no cliché can actually be a cliché. He remakes words.

Muldoon's poetry is mobile, sparking, and unrestrained in its venturings, though it is also deeply constrained by the manner of his journeying, who *he* is. There is an *it is* in the poetry, and a *he is* in its writing. The two don't map neatly over each other. Voice escapes and sets up its own realms of expression.

As a radically innovative formalist, Paul Muldoon's highly patterned and linguistically variable poetry is, as intimated, rarely 'didactic' for the sake of 'telling', and consequently, meaning is never stagnant. In an interview with Sean O'Brien (unpublished, 1994), Muldoon talked about how important clarity is for him; we need to differentiate between the intention of clarity in expression, and the potential for expansion and reinterpretation once the poetry is removed from its context. O'Brien also points out that place and context move for Muldoon at an alarming rate.[2] His poetry neither geographically nor conceptually occupies one zone. It's a liminal poetry that lives both sides of any given border – in some ways, his poetry is in an ongoing state of visitation with its roots in linguistic and cultural reassurance (bardic?). The personal (intensely at times) mixes with the overtly political, the generational (especially re. pleasure and excess and the mutual ability of language to synthesise a past moment, or bring an immediate awareness of a Wordsworthian spot of time, time not necessarily passed into memory), with the mythological. He fuses modes of expression that are as much about the need for language to express immediate concerns as they are about cultural and geographical necessity.

Language isn't just about words. The word 'muldoonery' has been coined to emphasise Muldoon's playfulness and inventiveness

---

2 Quotes from Sean O'Brien's unpublished interview with Paul Muldoon (1994) were used as an epigraph to 'The Advanced Muldoon', Chapter 17 of O'Brien's book *The Deregulated Muse: Essays on Contemporary British and Irish Poetry*, Newcastle Upon Tyne, Bloodaxe Books, 1998, p. 171.

with language, though it is often misunderstood to mean something light-hearted, almost ethereally amusing. But it is an unpicking of the vagaries of language, the potential for disaster that comes from imprecision. Maybe this is what Muldoon means when he talks of the relevance of 'clarity'. He needs to register the atomic changes of language, to observe, calibrate, keep track, realising the whole time that certainty is death, and that the dictionary is the graveyard, though he can't resist dipping in and out of it on an obsessive basis. This is why Muldoon's darker poems are irrepressible and alive – capturing the senses with their energetic wordplay before reconstituting in thought, bringing on that headache!

Paul Muldoon also makes innovative use of the poetic sequence. Be it lyrical cumulative, fragmentary, conversational, even displaced-narrative, there is always a sense of movement. A good example of the whole being greater than its parts would be his 'Hopewell Haiku' sequence from *Hay* (1998), and I include some sections from this below (which, along with a few other poems and extracts of poems, I have sneaked in via the backdoor of this introduction . . . but are not included in the collection per se):

V

A stone at its core,
this snowball's the porcelain
knob on winter's door.

VI

Our wild cat, Pangur,
spent last night under the hood
of my old banger.

VII

I tamped it with hay,
the boot that began to leak
Thursday or Friday.

A vigorous take on Basho-like accumulation, where the poet collaborates with a subconscious voice, an echo of self. The meditative moment of the haiku is cast in a cumulative lyric, simultaneously building a narrative. Muldoon is similarly inventive with sonnets, playing half-rhymes and internal rhymes, line lengths, and working the 'message' of the poem against the quirky diction. In other words, the poet is always experimental, even when the work is more readily accessible. In this selection, however, my criteria have been to show the range of his innovations, which become self-evident as the book unfolds – versatility of form and expression, clashes of irascible humour and cutting moral investigation (which he also concurrently undermines), the immense stability and solidity of the line with the explosive nature of words themselves: *ostranenie* ('genuine strangeness') for the time machine that is a Muldoon poem, from its most 'simple' to its most 'obtuse'.

We make use of the language of our experience to convey our poetic sympathies, our ideas, our intuitions and notions. In translating shared experience, especially that of family, into the public realm of the poem, we need a mediation point, an anchor that allows others to connect with the necessarily hermetic privacy of our experience. A word, a fetishised object – these can bring an awareness that informs our reading or hearing of the 'stranger's verse'. The poem is a way of saying the unsayable, of giving utterance to the private, without betraying the most private moment or knowledge. It works as artifice; it suggests an intimacy that cannot be replicated, the moment having passed. Or maybe a poem could be written in real time, like the photo capturing the daisy before it dies, keeping it that way in perpetuity? But the photo, like the poem, is a construct (or at least verges on being a construct), a translation of the experience or knowledge it conveys.

We see these apparent contradictions between familiarity and alienation, the desire to separate experiences yet also to wind them together to make sense of them, in, say, Muldoon's quite famous poem 'Quoof'. This poem skirts taboo, taking the family into an incestuous proximity to the sexual moment. The language of touch is as alien as the lack of language we assume between the protagonist and antagonist. Something as commonplace and 'real' as the water bottle becomes a transient object of change, a communication device, a thesaurus, and a way of attempting to resolve sexual tension and questions of invasiveness, which are impossible to resolve. It is simultaneously an object of comfort and bewilderment, even aggression. And the sound of the word itself 'quoof', echoes this. It is both exotic and commonplace in its immediacy. It seems to demand an etymology, though it is evasive; simple and complex at once. So, given this complexity of enactment and intent, the reader might ask why it is not included in this collection. In many ways, that is because it does not evade reading in the same way the poems from the same collection (*Quoof* (1983)) I have selected. The poem 'Glanders' (which is included!) works on the weight of a word and its origins-meaning ('glanders'), and also seems to have a fairly 'straight' linear delivery, but its weaving of tales tangential to the central conceit, of implication beyond what we can grasp through the poem, takes it into the realm of the neat yet unfulfilling fairy tale: its compaction and 'roll' (or as I term it at home, 'slaloming' through a Muldoon poem) that seem to tie all ends together, in fact splinter our perception of Larry Toal being 'so at ease with himself'. 'Quoof' might well have been included, but these slight differences in what surrounds the poem as points of departure from its 'narrative', are what, for me, differentiate in the context of this collection. But here is 'Quoof' by way of comparison:

How often have I carried our family word
for the hot water bottle
to a strange bed,
as my father would juggle a red-hot half-brick
in an old sock
to his childhood settle.
I have taken it into so many lovely heads
or laid it between us like a sword.

A hotel room in New York City
with a girl who spoke hardly any English,
my hand on her breast
like the smouldering one-off spoor of the yeti

or some other shy beast
that has yet to enter the language.

The hotel room might appear as alienated from home as one can get, but isn't *really* – how does this compare with the implied familiarity of the 'shaman' Larry Toal in 'Glanders'? A strange, familiarish but defamiliarising comfort. Are these two poems companion poems of a sort, or working as opposites? In 'Quoof', the transience of it undermines the sense of family and obligation to being a national, to being of a specific place, heritage and family, while retaining the emotional implications of that connection. Complex political statements are made here in a richly evocative and figurative way. The hot prints of desire in the indifferent snow; the tracks of love that will not be repeated, almost as if he shouldn't have gone there in the first place. The 'one-off' abominable spoor/spore is also, to the ear, biological and uncomfortable (ancient, potentially fungal and infectious). Its ability to colonise or impregnate the body of the gender-other, the geographical other, is offset by its suppressed sexual energy: 'smouldering'. But the lack of expression is made in the moment of doing, and the mystery (the unconfirmed existence of the yeti) generates a certainty, an emphasis. The 'smouldering' is troubling, but an affirmation of life, of energy. The poem is strangely threatening, yet enclosed as well. And we have the same 'enclosure' of the local being opened to threats of the outside world in 'Glanders', where even the familiar 'smoke' as part of the 'tranquil' setting of the healer-shaman's cottage is slightly nightmarish, slightly out of kilter and strange and threatening to the psyche if not the body. There's a Muldoonian paradox of the surreal bordering on the abject (a form of 'weirding', really) – the smoke coming down the chimney, 'tethering' the patient (healing as threat to body as well … or a psycho-homeopathy?) – the movement of the 'fairy tale' is reversed, flipped into the bizarre of the actual, the real. And 'Glanders' has certainties of belonging but with information coming from elsewhere, because the 'national' is not 'nationalistic', and language (and healing) are influenced by lines of communication and journeying. The body being healed is linked to the broader knowledge of the healer, his being a conduit for external as well as internal (local) experiences – a matrix of language as healing, but also where tradition meets presentiment, where things are stable and in flux. It is that last overwhelming stanza wherein the tension of the local in terms of the 'great' and small events of the outside world close in at that interstice where ignorance and knowledge meet, talking (as a hairdresser might do) as body repairs are done:

> for the mud of Flanders,
> how he came within that of the cure for glanders
> from a Suffolkman who suddenly went west.

That's the thing with Muldoon's poetry: it's like snapshots of the evolution of languages, and though cumulative and growing as an interactive oeuvre, each moment is a strange, completely organised snapshot.

This selection, being 'chronological', necessarily demonstrates conscious changes in epistemological and formal approaches to the writing of place, the ongoing impacts of colonisation, personal and communal loss, grief, rurality, the development and problems with 'Western thought' (as exemplified, most often, through their declarers – self-advertisers, maybe, for a take on the world ... utopias and idealisms founder, but language grows and in that is hope?), representation and misrepresentation of 'normative' sexuality, traditions of the courtly poem, traditions and confinements of religious poetry and poetry of adoration, slippages between poetry and realpolitik and global politics, the hybrid poetics and politics of Ireland-America as a literary construct and social reality, 'The Troubles', Irish independence and relationship to Britain (primarily 'England') – and the list continues. However, it's not a covering-of-all-possibilities kind of list, but a genuine engagement with intangibles and distresses, as well as celebratory engagements with music, people, nature, that in poetry resolves itself as an accumulation of observation and lexicality, a grand anaphora that is also a contents page to experience – not resolved, but constantly being considered, being voiced. And always throughout it, the humour that is particularly Muldoon's – yes, inflected with Beckettian bleakness in the face of the hole of self, and with a Joycean bawdiness (that word alone could be a way into muldoonery), and Moll Flanders in the wings and a troupe of players passing through the Village (rural or New York and wherever in the world, too!) ... specific, but internationalist, gender-evasive, the laughs of Paul Muldoon are wry.

I would argue that Muldoon's humour and devastating ironic wordplay (his 'muldoonery') are a means of critiquing a complex and contradictory 'world'. This is furthered by considering the 'riddling' techniques both as a means of confronting inequality and injustice through satire, irony and regular self-mockery, and also as a means of offering a moral agenda without 'forcing it down people's throats'. His reliance on the riddles of the Exeter Book, on traditions of wordplay in Irish (even of riddling techniques found in children's popular magazines of the 60s and 70s) is a way of bringing the reader to a point of self-analysis. We look to answer the riddle and find ourselves interrogating what we are as readers. The relationship between poet and reader is paramount in a Muldoon poem, especially in the post-*Hay* collections.

As part of that relationship, so often 'playfully' ironic, with the reader, Muldoon also occasionally seeks an intimacy in which his 'subject' is cherished even beyond the reach of language itself. When he uses an elegiac resistance, even 'blocking', a wordplay that 'distracts' from the pain of loss and phenomenological failure, the 'self' that creates and/or speaks the poem is the repository of a loss and anguish that can be overwhelming (loss of parents, child at birth, pivotal relationships, connections with the creativity of others). We might think of Mary Farl Powers, Seamus Heaney and many others in this light. The elegy is one of the main strands of Muldoon's poetry, but it is argued that this mode underpins all, even his love poems, which constantly confront the 'little deaths' of sex.

Religion and its controls are recurring concerns and subtext in the Muldoon lyric and his undoing of the lyric through 'play'. In a mirroring fashion, Muldoon presents constant alternatives to religion, and might at times be described as 'pagan' in his undoings and reconstitutions. Often, close readings of his poetry yield outcomes that are very far from the collective effect his poetry has – a book is a book for Muldoon: finishing a collection with a long poem, the use of smaller poems as a fulcrum (haiku, 'selfies' etc), the mixing of 'family' and memory poems with deconstructions (literally – a case for Derrida on writing is argued, also for signature and 'name' and the extension of play in writing in 'muldoonery' and the literal play on his name in the poetry over decades) – deconstructions of real-world vs popular culture are embedded in his collections as a modus operandi, and not an aesthetic choice. In many ways, Muldoon creates an anti-aesthetic, sometimes full of what a colleague describes as an 'artiness', which means he can only be read as innovative, even in his most apparently conventional lyrics.

Always pushing against constraints of language that can be 'understood' by a readership (any readership), Paul Muldoon has deployed a great variety of formal approaches to allowing a poem to voice itself. But by this I mean that, say, within a verse libretto such as *Shining Brow*, which is concerned with architect Frank Lloyd Wright's affair with a client's wife, there is a dramatic operatic presentation (fused with Daron Aric Hagen's music and originally performed by the Madison Opera company) of many voices, but there's also a thread of 'the poem' that runs throughout, with the language almost working around a fulcrum (even a 'maypole', if we want to introduce an awkward pun – the ribbons of lines running around the folk spine/pole of English-language ritualising to welcome the season of prosperity and hope . . . a terrible irony . . . but this is a generic observation, not a textually specific one!). This fulcrum is most often created by a chorus, and that is the case in this master poem as well (draftsmen/chorus), yet it's also the dichotomy of Wright's 'Public' and 'Private' voices conversing, it's the voice of 'ALL', it's the multiple reporters and photographers and workmen and townswomen. Class and privilege of speech are always variables in Muldoon's poetics. Herein is a key to Muldoon's innovations: no voice he conveys is intact, it is made up of fragments of many voices of reading and life experience, of bardic utterances and the many musicianships of humanity in nature: so much control, such formal constraints, and yet so many internal tensions. This is the paradox of Muldoon's poetics – his own voice is always questioning itself, and the voices of his poetry have voices conversing in layer on layer of 'themselves'. The dislocating self and dislocating selves.

WRIGHT

(*Public*)

> Ladies and gentlemen, let me take this occasion
> to welcome you to Taliesin.

(WRIGHT *reaches into his pocket to retrieve his prepared statement, from which he reads.*)

(*Public*)

> For seven long years I have withstood
> the slings and arrows
> of the fourth estate.
> I am a man of sorrow
> and acquainted with grief.
> It's fitting that, today of all days,
> I should most humbly crave
> your indulgence. Let me say my say.
>
> You know only too well
> the details of my private life,
> how a great misfortune befell
> myself and my wife,
>
> how we drifted further and further
> apart.
> Can a man be a faithful husband and father
> and devote himself to his art?

(*Private*)

> The truth is that I never
> gave Catherine her proper due.
> I have been a traitor
> to my wife, my friends, to architecture.

14

(Public)

> I was forced to choose. The choice
> I made
> gives me no cause to rejoice.
> My mouth is full of brine.

(Private)

> The truth is that I feel
> nothing, not the merest hint
> of remorse.
> Not a pang of guilt.

(Public)

> You know only too well
> what happened next. I was enthralled
> by this blessed damozel.

(WRIGHT *gestures towards* MAMAH.)

> She pierced my heart like an arrowhead.

(Private)

> The truth is that I have been cruel.
> There is a hardness in my heart.
> I have torn down
> many beautiful things.
>
> The truth is that I am by nature cast
> in the role of the iconoclast.
> I have torn down
> much that was beautiful.
>
> The truth is that I have been cruel.
> The truth is that I myself
> am the hump-backed whale.
> My mouth is full of krill.

Can a man be a faithful husband and father
and devote himself to his art?
The truth is that my back is to the wall.

(*Public*)

Our love is seen as a serious upheaval
of 'conventional' mores.
I'm 'the very embodiment of evil',
she's 'no better than a common whore'.

So much for the 'conventional'. The average
man may live by average laws;
the artist, however, must forge
in his own maw

some new vision of order,
an even more exacting moral code.
The artist must take a harder
and higher road,

through the dark night
of the soul towards a necessary light.

(*Private*)

The truth is that my back is to the wall.
The truth, the truth . . .

(*Public*)

That necessary light comes from within;
from there, and there alone.
For seven long years we have been prey
to rumours and allegations.

I prithee now; *Let him who is without sin*
cast the first stone.
Let it lodge in the 'Shining Brow'
of Taliesin.

16

For, just as Taliesin is not 'on', but 'of',
a gently sloping hill,
so my love
for Mamah Cheney is truly integral.

This is our Avalon.
This is our Chapel of the Holy Grail.

(WRIGHT *begins to fold his prepared speech.*)

(*Public*)

Now, ladies and gentlemen, we wish you all
a very merry
Christmas. We hope you will
join us in a glass of sherry,
here in this house that hill
might marry.

(*Shining Brow*, Faber & Faber, London, 1993, pp. 45–8)

And the search for utopias against their inevitable failures is shown alongside some people's refusal to differentiate the nationalist and national, the settler and the colonised, the prophet and the poet, the entertainer and the commentator. Muldoon's writing life has been a search for mediums in which to synthesise – or, really, ironically and paradoxically, *polysynthesise* as he is always searching for new ways and methodologies – his fragmented vision (necessarily so because of conflict/s and dystopias), and *Madoc: A Mystery* (1990), a poetry sequence for which there are few comparisons (and few comparable achievements in poetry), is one of those points of innovation that carries consequences for reader and poet.

Potential questions around Muldoon's deployment of Native American (and other 'native') motifs, facts and literary representations in the context of the oppression of the Irish by English/British colonialists are explored in the present book through an extensive selection from his masterpiece, *Madoc: A Mystery* (more on this shortly). The selection here is intended to retain a

17

'narrative' (of Muldoon's original) while highlighting the linguistically challenging threads. Southey (of course) and Coleridge are 'well represented', but so are the diversions of quotation and language that help us understand how he is working against appropriation of Native American material, and not 'representing' without being aware of consequences. This is a work seeking to unravel the colonial thought-lines and desire lines – a challenging to the maps of conquest. In fact, it is argued that Muldoon's poetry is so consciously metatextual that he is willing to challenge all approaches to cultural issues in order to highlight the fact that problems will always exist in the presentation of cultural history, as there will always be an othering, and always an 'outside'. Muldoon makes no claim for insider privilege, outside his wide and declared deployment of 'Western' referents and data, but is examining the way language allows us to reconsider (as well as entrap us if we are vigilant with and at its forces).

The range of Muldoon's technical achievement is staggering. He has taken traditional Irish poetry (in Irish), the poetry of post-plantation Ireland, and Irish independence, and of pre-independence and post-independence 'Troubles', and reinvented it within a universalising 'english' that has almost become a language in itself. Not since James Joyce has there been such an everything-in-existence inclusiveness, with the deadly wry confrontation of emptiness, ennui and pointlessness that we might associate with Beckett or even the absurdity of Flann O'Brien. Further, Muldoon has taken the traditions of English-language poetry as it twists away from its centres through W. B. Yeats's work, has fractured its lyrical feedings on myth and tradition, and made it something new and potent for 'our times'. Muldoon's experiments with the sonnet have yielded a 'pattern poem' that is never thematically or intellectually constrained in its formal precision, but has become as versatile as a Shakespearean or Petrarchan sonnet. The Muldoon sonnet is an experimental closed form that offers infinite linguistic (words themselves) variations.

The use of conceit/fallacy/analogy to build what is often a polymorphously perverse Georgic shows how near and far he is from models such as Virgil. Many poems deploy metonym to build allusion and connection at once; it might be argued that a reinvigorated poetic structuralism is often at work masquerading as a post-structuralist play. Muldoon's poetry has its cake and eats it too, and belongs to no school. It is its own school, and seems to have many imitators! It is unique, and this uniqueness is used to challenge the reader's givens, their expectations. The world is not as we think, we learn. Also, what we accept as 'English', with its (Borg-like) ability to absorb and adapt (as all languages do, but markedly in the case of a colonial tongue), to build a dictionary out of loan words, to take on rules outside its previous experience, is tested to the extreme in Muldoon's poetry, and something other-than-English is created. How do we read a language? Whether through an almost-parataxis that convinces us we are reading a narrative when we are not, or a slippage into a portmanteau word that seems the logical word, the reader is taken for a ride through the unfamiliar made familiar. Muldoon, in dealing with the complexities (and horrors and beauties) of the real world, has created a paracosm that is nonetheless gritty, disturbing and challenging to what we assume is 'reality'.

The dialogue between art and life grows exponentially across the books, from artworks with personal associations (paintings, films) to the most fetishised and distanced commodifications of 'art'. How do we commune with the facile and make something resonant, even 'spiritual', from it? The 'quotidian' is much discussed by Muldoon critics, but the exoticism of the familiar is considered as a distancing and alienating trope here. Tangentially speaking, the place of Rosencrantz and Guildenstern in a play within a play (or rather, poems within poems), of *Waiting for Godot*, of dandyism, ennui and the power and contradictions of 'rock music' – all are brought into play in one form or another.

In defence of some of my choices in the context of innovation, I offer a few brief notes. Regarding 'Epona' from *Mules* (1977) – this is an early love-sex-play allusion poem re conventions of the courtly. The poems from *Quoof* (1983) are pivotal (and 'Quoof' itself was first chosen in my earliest version of this selection) – as with the selections from the earlier collections, poems here are chosen to show a gathering experimentalism, a searching for linguistic, prosodic and even thematic approaches that liberate the

19

poem from the traditions it speaks with and also resists: a new methodology for approaching the writing of poems is evolving not out of 'choice' so much as 'necessity'. I am fascinated by 'From Strength to Strength', which convinces me as a pro-animal rights poem, in its essence. Interesting here is that Muldoon is sometimes critiqued as using the 'natural world' in a utilitarian fashion in his language constructions, but it can be argued that even the most matter-of-fact reference to eating/cooking/usage of animals comes laden with implication of cause and effect. And 'Yggdrasill' might be considered as a 'transitional' poem wherein various historical/ literary/found modes come into play.

Meeting the British (1987) was a turning-point collection in terms of new approaches to lyric and innovation. 'My Grandfather's Wake' is a poem of family that works through digression, juxtaposition, and sidestepping emotional pain, as seen later in the poem for his sister in Horse Latitudes (2006), where 'metastasis' reaches right through the poet himself, the reader and language itself, altering the nature of that language. 'The Mist-Net' (originally in Wishbone for artist Mary Farl Powers) seems indelible to me. And I should mention the eponymous 'Meeting the British', which was another early inclusion because of not formal but conceptual innovation. This poem becomes a political/ethical template regarding other colonial enactments and their consequences ('contact', a politics of language usage and usurping, exponential competing and conflicting (French/British) colonialisms and their consequences, the falsity of 'manners', theft of Indigenous lands, sickness... death). The political impetus that has been gathering and progresses exponentially from this work on, in terms of resisting the colonial, the matter-of-fact of the quotidian mixed with empire-narrative-horror, all constrained, packaged and presented. I quote it here:

> We met the British in the dead of winter.
> The sky was lavender
>
> and the snow lavender-blue.
> I could hear, far below,

the sound of two streams coming together
(both were frozen over)

and, no less strange,
myself calling out in French

across that forest-
clearing. Neither General Jeffrey Amherst

nor Colonel Henry Bouquet
could stomach our willow-tobacco.

As for the unusual
scent when the Colonel shook out his hand-

kerchief: *C'est la lavande,*
une fleur mauve comme le ciel.

They gave us six fishhooks
and two blankets embroidered with smallpox.

If we, as Muldoon, depart from Robert Southey's faux-epic
pseudo-historical *Madoc* (1805)[3] which he hoped would help fund

---

3 Southey's 'Preface' to Volume One (of two) of *Madoc* (1805), concludes
with the words: 'The manner of the Poem, in both its parts, will be
found historically true. It assumes not the degraded title of Epic; and
the question, therefore, is not whether the story is formed upon the
rules of Aristotle, but whether it be adapted to the purposes of poetry.'
Keep in mind that we are talking of a 'legendary' twelfth-century
Welsh king (with Irish connections) adventuring to the Americas
where he pursues a better life – 'the land which he discovered
pleased him' (and the 'Aztecas, an American tribe' of the place,
concurrently began a *shift* from 'calamity' and (ill)-'omen' to move
to another place and 'became a mighty people, and founded the
Mexican empire'). Southey's detailed use of 'source materials' and
intertexuality (his notes are extensive), is as much in play as paratext
(Genette) as Muldoon's various thinker-'voices'-mediators/narratorial
foci (and at one point in the full poem, 'Aristotle' conveys/marks a

his Pantisocratic[4] life in (the) America(s), and segue with migration, diaspora and the failure of utopias, then we have a context for Part Two of *Madoc: A Mystery* (1990) through which to tackle Muldoon's failure of history and mythology in terms of what a (fragmenting epic) poem might contain. I have always been intrigued by the constantly eroding distance between author and subject in this work, and the relationship between Welsh and Irish iconographies as mediated through English-language romanticism and ideas of 'America' – the seismic consequences of 'Western' thinking and colonial compulsions, and the internal contradictions of creative, political and economic utopianism. Though we might more readily equate 'muldoonery' with S. T. Coleridge than Southey, there's also an 'earnest' motivation behind Muldoon's work. Consider Richard Holmes's observations in *Coleridge: Early Visions, 1772–1804* (1989/2005): 'While Southey wrote long, apocalyptic letters prophesying violent revolution in England, and urging his friends to join him in Kentucky (the first site for Pantisocracy), Coleridge adopted an altogether lighter touch. The difference in tone here was already significant, for there was always an element of humorous fantasy in Coleridge's Pantisocracy which quite escaped Southey's earnestness' (p. 64). For a scheme of youth (with genuinely radical commitments to liberty and fairness, however gender-skewed these might have been) which never actually happened, and which remained a form of utopian colonial displacement fantasia of the volatile Euro-years

---

quote from Southey) cross-reference 'each other'. See https://books. google.com.au/books?id=JiYhAAAAMAAJ&printsec=frontcover&dq= intitle:Madoc&hl=en&ei=Gp4_TczLEt2L4gaT9bGQAw&sa=X&oi=book_ result&ct=result&redir_esc=y#v=onepage&q&f=false.

4 Some of the 'players' might be amused to see the (American) Oxford Dictionary define Pantisocracy as: 'Pantisocracy | ˌpantɪˈsɒkrəsi | noun [mass noun] a form of utopian social organization in which all are equal in social position and responsibility'. For an enlightening biographical encounter with Southey, Coleridge and the others in their youthful zest (so remarkably 'undone' and 'redone' via Muldoon in *Madoc*) through the focal point of Coleridge's life, see Richard Holmes's *Coleridge: Early Visions, 1772–1804* (1989/2005).

of 1793–4, with sisters/friends/poetry/radicalism all in the mix, it is not surprising Muldoon has used this as an explosive undoing of persistent colonial fantasising ('set' along the Susquehanna River).

The Annals of Chile (1994) is another tour-de-force, with poems such as 'Incantata', which may not be specifically 'innovative' but is certainly lyrically digressive with its working of allusion and counterpoint. It amplifies in the context of earlier Mary Farl Powers material. And in Part Two's 'That was the year...', we are homing in on an 'event' and its never letting go, however far away the mental and physical travels and travails take the poet-persona.

A favourite of mine is the maybe lesser-known collection of Muldoon's, his 'January journal', *The Prince of the Quotidian* (1994). Thinking of 'Much as I'm taken', I automatically compare the conjugation play with the seriousness of the conjugation play in *Horse Latitudes'* (2006) 'Hedge School', a poem not overtly experimental but one whose essence symbolically reaches back and forth through all the work. Loss – personal loss and loss for humanity – impels language-play, the materiality and cost of meaning in 'the word itself' across cultural spaces, across languages, across bodies and their vulnerabilities to colonisation and 'conquest': 'forced to conjugate/ *Guantánamo, amas, amat*' and *'metastasis'*. History's consequences are invasively *now*.

From *Horse Latitudes,* I have also included 'The Outlier' because of the iteration of the belonging/alienation binary issue ('I fell between two stones' and 'they prised and propped open') as a strand of Muldoon's variations and innovations of traditional forms; and there's the red herring of literary interpretation in the 'The Mountain is Holding Out' (conceit or not?). I cannot resist the innovative wryness in the song lyricism of *General Admission* (2006) – the guitar close to the song-poem, and its singing – in which the witty retort is embedded in the pop cultural catch-all that rocks along. As someone suggested to me, the emphasis is on the *stanza* in the song: stanzas as much as verses.

'Plan B' appeared in a book published by Enitharmon with stark and evocative 'juxtaposition' (as I think of them) images by photographer Norman McBeath of whom Muldoon wrote in the introduction, 'He has that rare ability to allow nothing, least of all himself, to come between the subject of a photograph and the perceiver. That holds true of a sheep or a statue of Apollo in transit; the medium does not hold a sense of mediation. There is, rather, an invitation to *meditate*. The very idea of a "subject" soon begins to seem crudely inappropriate' (*Plan B*, 2009). Yes, so we juxtapose and watch and listen to poem and photograph, and we don't impose, or try not to. Later appearing in *Maggot* (2010), the sequence 'Plan B' appears sans photos and becomes an equally brilliant sequence of the visual, of cruelty and exploitation in the story of Topsy the Elephant, New World as construct and fantasia . . .

But 'Plan B' was born out of collaboration with a photographer, and as poet-musician, Muldoon has increasingly collaborated with others. He has lone versions of his work, and 'together'/shared versions of his work. They are different forms of the 'same', always intersecting. Again, I ask what constitutes the 'innovative', and always I arrive at acts of dislocation between self and subject, intent and what language does itself regardless . . . maybe it's 'crudely inappropriate' to apply conditions of expectation when reading? In *One Thousand Things Worth Knowing* (2015), 'The Firing Squad' might be demi/semi-experimental; this-is-what-you-died -for irony; self-sacrifice and killing working against form? I find myself in the audience listening to the lead singer, but also closely following each member of the band, always wondering how a song written by one person is constructed in the shared context.

So, what we have here is a personal selection of poetry I see as linguistically innovative not just because of disruptions of syntax and 'ambiguous' *meaning*, but sometimes for elusive reasons outside these quantifiers of experimentation. More often, there's an essential quiddity, a subtle turn in meaning and expression that lifts the poem outside its times and even context, and leaves me wondering where and how it sits in his oeuvre. That is necessarily subjective, but this selection is, for me, an embodiment of a readerly experience with the complexities of Paul Muldoon's verbal sophistication and prosody as they accord with complex meanings. Muldoon *is* a maverick who nonetheless exists in parallel to, say, the construct of a Cambridge School of linguistically-politically concerned poetics (he was actually Judith E. Wilson Fellow in poetry in the Cambridge University English Faculty, and his poetry is widely read, discussed and written about there) and (again, 'say') the American Language Poets, from whom he is definitively *apart*, but with whom he shares some overlap in approach to language in times of trauma, and seeing the poem as an act of commitment.

The gaps between secular and religious verse, between rationalism and empiricism, liturgy/hymns and legal language, are twisted into immeasurables in Muldoon's poetry as he pushes it to converse with all *language*, as he wrestles with dislocations. Paul Muldoon's poetic language attempts to converse across cultural spaces – not intrusively, but passionately with interest, respect and even wonder. He is an internationalist with a very specific and necessary sense of origins and translocation – a traveller who encounters and feeds his language-reservoir with exposure to other linguistic conversations and knowledges. His seems a belief in the infinite capacity of language to take the stress of increase in order to focus on the local and specific. His modus operandi can be truly generous, and ultimately shamanistic and healing. He travels and travels again . . . and is in awe and wonder at eagles and camels and the conversations of people around them in specific locales; his ability to resist the constraints of his inherited and learnt technique offers space in the poem of his own construction for genuine conversation with what is not his to 'own'. It's a living and growing poetry, and never a closed-off poetry. Thus this is no closed book, and cannot be made one. This is a collection without closure.

A new or fresh engagement with Muldoon's poetry will excite readers as they (re)encounter his 'sprung syntax' (best term I can conjure), demi-parataxis, faux-colloquial diversions (mixed with the genuinely colloquial he picks up as he travels and as he sits and listens to local chat), traditional forms accelerated into a vigorous newness, rhyme that is expected but also sudden and always surprising and that leaps across lines and kerns lines as well, and attendant stunning tricks of enjambment. Muldoon's formal dexterity leaves the reader stunned. But these prosodic innovations are only the 'obvious' part of his innovative poetics – so much of what is radical in Muldoon is the bulk of linguistic implication that 'icebergs' below the surface, that reflects tensions, intricacies and convolutions of life on the surface. In both joy and loss, in surprise and resistance, there always seems to be songs, chants and intoning going on across and between Muldoon poems – mostly I hear the *Te Deum*, but there are many.

Poems

The Electric Orchard

The early electric people had domesticated the wild ass.
They knew all about falling off.
Occasionally, they would have fallen out of the trees.
Climbing again, they had something to prove
To their neighbours. And they did have neighbours.
The electric people lived in villages
Out of their need of security and their constant hunger.
Together they would divert their energies

To neutral places. Anger to the banging door,
Passion to the kiss.
And electricity to earth. Having stolen his thunder
From an angry god, through the trees
They had learned to string his lightning.
The women gathered random sparks into their aprons,
A child discovered the swing
Among the electric poles. Taking everything as given,

The electric people were confident, hardly proud.
They kept fire in a bucket,
Boiled water and dry leaves in a kettle, watched the lid
By the blue steam lifted and lifted.
So that, where one of the electric people happened to fall,
It was accepted as an occupational hazard.
There was something necessary about the thing. The North Wall

Of the Eiger was notorious for blizzards,
If one fell there his neighbour might remark, Bloody fool.
All that would have been inappropriate,
Applied to the experienced climber of electric poles.
I have achieved this great height?
No electric person could have been that proud,

Thirty or forty feet. Perhaps not that,
If the fall happened to be broken by the roof of a shed.
The belt would burst, the call be made,

The ambulance arrive and carry the faller away
To hospital with a scream.
There and then the electric people might invent the railway,
Just watching the lid lifted by the steam.
Or decide that all laws should be based on that of gravity,
Just thinking of the faller fallen.
Even then they were running out of things to do and see.
Gradually, they introduced legislation

Whereby they nailed a plaque to every last electric pole.
They would prosecute any trespassers.
The high up, singing and live fruit liable to shock or kill
Were forbidden. Deciding that their neighbours
And their neighbours' innocent children ought to be stopped
For their own good, they threw a fence
Of barbed wire round the electric poles. None could describe
Electrocution, falling, the age of innocence.

The Glad Eye

Bored by Ascham and Zeno
In private conversation on the longbow,

I went out onto the lawn.
Taking the crooked bow of yellow cane,

I shot an arrow over
The house and wounded my brother.

He cried those huge dark tears
Till they had blackened half his hair.

Zeno could have had no real
Notion of the flying arrow being still,

Not blessed with the hindsight
Of photography and the suddenly frozen shot,

Yet that obstinate one
Eye inveigled me to a standing stone.

Evil eyes have always burned
Corn black and people have never churned

Again after their blink.
That eye was deeper than the Lake of the Young,

Outstared the sun in the sky.
Could look without commitment into another eye.

Clonfeacle

It happened not far away
In this meadowland
That Patrick lost a tooth.
I translate the placename

As we walk along
The river where he washed,
That translates stone to silt.
The river would preach

As well as Patrick did.
A tongue of water passing
Between teeth of stones.
Making itself clear,

Living by what it says,
Converting meadowland to marsh.
You turn towards me,
Coming round to my way

Of thinking, holding
Your tongue between your teeth.
I turn my back on the river
And Patrick, their sermons

Ending in the air.

Lunch with Pancho Villa

I

'Is it really a revolution, though?'
I reached across the wicker table
With another $10,000 question.
My celebrated pamphleteer,
Co-author of such volumes
As *Blood on the Rose,*
The Dream and the Drums,
And *How It Happened Here,*
Would pour some untroubled Muscatel
And settle back in his cane chair.

'Look, son. Just look around you.
People are getting themselves killed
Left, right and centre
While you do what? Write rondeaux?
There's more to living in this country
Than stars and horses, pigs and trees,
Not that you'd guess it from your poems.
Do you never listen to the news?
You want to get down to something true,
Something a little nearer home.'

I called again later that afternoon,
A quiet suburban street.
'You want to stand back a little
When the world's at your feet.'
I'd have liked to have heard some more
Of his famous revolution.
I rang the bell, and knocked hard
On what I remembered as his front door,
That opened then, as such doors do,
Directly on to a back yard.

II

Not any back yard, I'm bound to say,
And not a thousand miles away
From here. No one's taken in, I'm sure,
By such a mild invention.
But where (I wonder myself) do I stand,
In relation to a table and chair,
The quince-tree I forgot to mention,
That suburban street, the door, the yard—
All made up as I went along
As things that people live among.

And such a person as lived there!
My celebrated pamphleteer!
Of course, I gave it all away
With those preposterous titles.
The Bloody Rose? *The Dream and the Drums*?
The three-day-wonder of the flowering plum!
Or was I desperately wishing
To have been their other co-author,
Or, at least, to own a first edition
Of *The Boot Boys and Other Battles*?

'When are you going to tell the truth?'
For there's no such book, so far as I know,
As *How it Happened Here*,
Though there may be. There may.
What should I say to this callow youth
Who learned to write last winter—
One of those correspondence courses—
And who's coming to lunch today?
He'll be rambling on, no doubt,
About pigs and trees, stars and horses.

Epona

I have no heart, she cries. I am driving her madder,
Out of her depth, almost, in the tall grass
Of Parsons' triangular meadow.
Because I straddle some old jackass

Whose every hoof curves like the blade
Of a scythe. It staggers over
Towards a whitethorn hedge, meaning to rid
Itself of me. Just in time, I slither

Off the sagging, flabbergasted back.
To calm a jackass, they say, you take its ear like a snaffle
Between your teeth. I bite her ear and shoo her back
Into the middle of my life.

Boon

'And what's the snow that melts the soonest?'
Mercy was thirteen, maybe fourteen.
'And how would you catch a yellow bittern?'
She was half-way down the mountainside

Before I'd realised. 'I would be right glad
If you knew next Sunday.' Her parting shot
Left me more intent than Lancelot
Upon the Grail. Or whoever it was. Sir Galahad.

'A yellow bittern?' I'd consulted Will Hunter,
Who carried a box of matches
And had gone by himself to the pictures.
He wrinkled his nose. 'I know green linnets

You take with just a pinch of salt
On their tails. That's according to most people.
A yellow bittern. They might be special.'
'And the snow that's first to melt?'

I'd got that wrong. He was almost certain.
'The snow that scarcely ever lies
Falls on a lady's breasts and thighs.'
That week stretched longer than the Creation!

We climbed the hills to the highest hill-farm
Without a word of snow or bittern
And viewed the extravagant wilderness
Of the brawling townlands round the Moy,

The cries from the football-field grown so dim
We might be listening on the wireless.
When I'd all but forgotten that she'd forgotten
Mercy would take me in her arms.

Promises, Promises

I am stretched out under the lean-to
Of an old tobacco-shed
On a farm in North Carolina.
A cardinal sings from the dogwood
For the love of marijuana.
His song goes over my head.
There is such splendour in the grass
I might be the picture of happiness.
Yet I am utterly bereft
Of the low hills, the open-ended sky,
The wave upon wave of pasture
Rolling in, and just as surely
Falling short of my bare feet.
Whatever is passing is passing me by.

I am with Raleigh, near the Atlantic,
Where we have built a stockade
Around our little colony.
Give him his scallop-shell of quiet,
His staff of faith to walk upon,
His scrip of joy, immortal diet—
We are some eighty souls
On whom Raleigh will hoist his sails.
He will return, years afterwards,
To wonder where and why
We might have altogether disappeared,
Only to glimpse us here and there
As one fair strand in her braid,
The blue in an Indian girl's dead eye.

I am stretched out under the lean-to
Of an old tobacco-shed
On a farm in North Carolina,
When someone or other, warm, naked,
Stirs within my own skeleton
And stands on tip-toe to look out
Over the horizon,
Through the zones, across the ocean.
The cardinal sings from a redbud
For the love of one slender and shy,
The flight after flight of stairs
To her room in Bayswater,
The damson freckle on her throat
That I kissed when we kissed Goodbye.

Mary Farl Powers: *Pink Spotted Torso*

I

She turns from the sink
potato in hand. A Kerr's Pink,
its water-dark
port-wine birthmark
that will answer her knife
with a hieroglyph.

II

The open book of Minnesota
falls open at Main Street, an almost total
sky, sweet nothings in the Soda
Fountain, joy-
rides among the tidal
wheat-fields, midnight swims with the Baumgartner boy.

You saw through that flooded granite quarry
to the wreckage of an Oldsmobile,
saw, never more clearly,
him unmanacle
himself from buckled steel, from the weight of symbol,
only to be fettered by an ankle.

Glanders

When you happened to sprain your wrist or ankle
you made your way to the local shaman,
if 'shaman' is the word for Larry Toal,
who was so at ease with himself, so tranquil,

a cloud of smoke would graze on his thatch
like the cow in the cautionary tale,
while a tether of smoke curled down his chimney
and the end of the tether was attached

to Larry's ankle or to Larry's wrist.
He would conjure up a poultice of soot and spit
and flannel-talk, how he had a soft spot

for the mud of Flanders,
how he came within that of the cure for glanders
from a Suffolkman who suddenly went west.

From Strength to Strength

A Charolais, the new cow-calf
will plunge out of her own shadow
as if from the bath.

Her bath towel
is a rich brocade.
She pummels herself. A talcum-rime.

She wants to meet the full-length
mirror head-on.
She is palmed off by the meadow,

me, my aluminium bucket.
She takes her milk like medicine.
Though she may lift her fraying tail

to skitter-dung,
she goes from strength to strength,
a gasping, veal-pale tongue.

Yggdrasill

From below, the waist-thick pine
seemed to arch
its back. It is a birch,
perhaps. At any rate, I could discern
a slight curvature of the spine.

They were gathered in knots
to watch me go.
A pony fouled the hard-packed snow
with her glib cairn,
someone opened a can of apricots.

As I climb
my nose is pressed to the bark.
The mark
of a cigarette burn
from your last night with him.

A snapshot of you and your sister
walking straight
through 1958,
The Works of Laurence Sterne
your only aid to posture.

The air is aerosol-
blue and chill. I have notched
up your pitch-
pine scent and the maidenhair fern's
spry arousal.

And it would be just swell and dandy
to answer
them with my tonsure,
to return
with the black page from *Tristram Shandy*.

Yet the lichened
tree trunk will taper
to a point where one scrap of paper
is spiked, and my people yearn
for a legend:

It may not be today
or tomorrow, but sooner or later
the Russians will water
their horses on the shores of Lough Erne
and Lough Neagh.

Ontario

I spent last night in the nursery of a house in Pennsylvania. When I put out the light I made my way, barefoot, through the aftermath of Brandywine Creek. The constellations of the northern hemisphere were picked out in luminous paint on the ceiling. I lay under a comforting, phosphorescent Plough, thinking about where the Plough stopped being the Plough and became the Big Dipper. About the astronomer I met in Philadelphia who had found a star with a radio telescope. The star is now named after her, whatever her name happens to be. As all these stars grew dim, it seemed like a good time to rerun my own dream-visions. They had flashed up just as I got into bed on three successive nights in 1972. The first was a close-up of a face, Cox's face, falling. I heard next morning how he had come home drunk and taken a nose-dive down the stairs. Next, my uncle Pat's face, falling in slo-mo like the first, but bloody. It turned out he had slipped off a ladder on a building-site. His forehead needed seven stitches. Lastly, a freeze-frame trickle of water or glycerine on a sheet of smoked glass or perspex. I see it in shaving-mirrors. Dry Martinis. Women's tears. On windshields. As planes take off or land. I remembered how I was meant to fly to Toronto this morning, to visit my younger brother. He used to be a research assistant at the University of Guelph, where he wrote a thesis on nitrogen-fixing in soya beans, or symbiosis, or some such mystery. He now works for the Corn Producers' Association of Ontario. On my last trip we went to a disco in the Park Plaza, where I helped a girl in a bin-liner dress to find her contact-lens.

—Did you know that Spinoza was a lens-grinder?

—Are you for real?

Joe was somewhere in the background, sniggering, flicking cosmic dandruff from his shoulders.

—A lens, I went on, is really a lentil. A pulse.

Her back was an imponderable green furrow in the ultraviolet strobe.

—Did *you* know that Yonge Street's the longest street in the world?

—I can't say that I did.

—Well, it starts a thousand miles to the north, and it ends right here.

My Grandfather's Wake

If the houses in Wyeth's Christina's dream
and Malick's *Days of Heaven*
are triremes, yes,
triremes riding the 'sea of grain',
then each has a little barge
in tow—a freshly-dug grave.

I was trying to remember, Nancy,
how many New England graveyards you own,
all silver birch
and neat white picket-fences.

If only that you might make room
for a nine-banded armadillo
found wandering in Meath
sometime in the 1860s;
a man-ox, a fish with three gold teeth
described by Giraldus Cambrensis.

Our cow chained in the byre
was a galley-slave from *Ben Hur*
to the old-fashioned child of seven
they had sent in search of a bucket of steam.

Gold

For Gerard Quinn

You loomed like Merlin
over the class
of 1962,

your soutane-
pocket like the scar
of an appendectomy.

—

Just a year earlier
old Frost
had swung the lead

while hailing Kennedy—
*A golden age
of poetry and power.*

—

Twenty years on you reach
into the breast
of a wind-cheater

for your blue pencil:
'All cancelled;
Nothing gold can stay.'

—

Not the dead weight
of a grouse
flaunted from an open car.

Not Soutine's
Hare on a Green Shutter.
Not Marilyn.

The Mist-Net

Though he checked the mist-net
every day for a month

he caught only two tiny birds;
one Pernod-sip,

one tremulous crème-de-menthe;
their tiny sobs

were his mother's dying words:
You mustn't. You mustn't.

from 7, Middagh Street

Quinquereme of Nineveh from distant Ophir;
a blizzard off the Newfoundland coast
had, as we slept, metamorphosed

the *Champlain*'s decks
to a wedding cake,
on whose uppermost tier stood Christopher

and I like a diminutive bride and groom.
A heavy-skirted Liberty would lunge
with her ice-cream
at two small, anxious

boys, and Erika so grimly wave
from the quarantine-launch
she might as truly have been my wife
as, later that day, Barcelona was Franco's.

—

There was a time when I thought it mattered
what happened in Madrid

or Seville
and, in a sense, I haven't changed
my mind; the forces of Good and Evil
were indeed ranged

against each other, though not unambiguously.
I went there on the off-chance
they'd let me try
my hand at driving an ambulance;

there turned out to be some bureau-
cratic hitch.
When I set out for the front on a black burro
it promptly threw me in the ditch.

I lay there for a year, disillusioned, dirty,
until a firing-party

of Chinese soldiers
came by, leading dishevelled ponies.
They arranged a few sedimentary boulders
over the body of a Japanese

spy they'd shot
but weren't inclined to bury,
so that one of his feet stuck out.
When a brindled pariah

began to gnaw
on it, I recognized the markings of the pup
whose abscessed paw
my father had lanced on our limestone doorstep.

—

Those crucial years he tended
the British wounded

in Egypt, Gallipoli
and France, I learned to play

Isolde to my mother's Tristan.
Are they now tempted to rechristen

their youngest son
who turned his back on Albion

a Quisling?
Would their *chaise-longue*

philosophers have me somehow inflate
myself and float

above their factories and pylons
like a flat-footed barrage-balloon?

—

For though I would gladly return to Eden
as that ambulance-driver
or air-raid warden
I will never again ford the river
to parley with the mugwumps
and fob them off with monocles and mumps;
I will not go back as *Auden*.

—

And were Yeats living at this hour
it should be in some ruined tower

not malachited Ballylee
where he paid out to those below

one gilt-edged scroll from his pencil
as though he were part-Rapunzel

and partly Delphic oracle.
As for his crass, rhetorical

posturing, 'Did that play of mine
send out certain men (*certain* men?)

the English shot . . .?'
the answer is 'Certainly not'.

If Yeats had saved his pencil-lead
would certain men have stayed in bed?

For history's a twisted root
with art its small, translucent fruit

and never the other way round.
The roots by which we were once bound

are severed here, in any case,
and we are all now dispossessed;

prince, poet, construction worker,
salesman, soda fountain jerker—

all equally isolated.
Each loads flour, sugar and salted

beef into a covered wagon
and strikes out for his Oregon,

each straining for the ghostly axe
of a huge, blond-haired lumberjack.

—

'If you want me look for me under your boot-soles';
when I visited him in a New Hampshire hospital
where he had almost gone for a Burton
with peritonitis
Louis propped himself up on an ottoman
and read aloud the ode to Whitman
from *Poeta en Nueva York*.
The impossible Eleanor Clark
had smuggled in a pail of oysters and clams
and a fifth column
of Armagnac.
Carson McCullers extemporized a blues harmonica
on urinous pipkins and pannikins
that would have flummoxed Benjamin Franklin.
I left them, so, to the reign
of the ear of corn
and the journey-work of the grass-leaf
and found my way next morning to Bread Loaf
and the diamond-shaped clearing in the forest
where I learned to play softball with Robert Frost.

—

For I have leapt with Kierkegaard
out of the realm of Brunel and Arkwright

with its mills, canals and railway-bridges
into this great void
where Chester and I exchanged love-pledges
and vowed
our marriage-vows. As he lay asleep
last night the bronze of his exposed left leg
made me want nothing so much as to weep.
I thought of the terrier, of plague,

of Aschenbach at the Lido.
Here was my historical
Mr W. H., my 'onlie begetter' and fair lady;
for nothing this wide universe I call . . .

SALVADOR

This lobster's not a lobster but the telephone
that rang for Neville Chamberlain.

It droops from a bare branch
above a plate, on which the remains of lunch

include a snapshot of Hitler
and some boiled beans left over

from *Soft Construction: A Premonition
of Civil War.* When Breton

hauled me before his kangaroo-court
I quoted the Manifesto; we must disregard

moral and aesthetic considerations
for the integrity of our dream-visions.

What if I dreamed of Hitler as a masochist
who raises his fist

only to be beaten?
I might have dreamed of fucking André Breton

he so pooh-poohed my *Enigma of William Tell.*
There I have Lenin kneel

with one massive elongated buttock
and the elongated peak

of his cap supported by two forked sticks.
This time there's a raw beef-steak

on the son's head. My father croons a lullaby.
Is it that to refer, however obliquely,

is to refer? In October 1934,
I left Barcelona by the back door

with a portfolio of work
for my first one-man show in New York.

A starry night. The howling of dogs.
The Anarchist taxi-driver carried two flags,

Spanish and Catalan. Which side was I on?
Not one, or both, or none.

I who had knelt with Lenin in Breton's court
and sworn allegiance to the proletariat

had seen the chasm
between myself and surrealism

begin as a hair-crack on a tile.
In *Soft Construction* I painted a giant troll

tearing itself apart limb
by outlandish limb.

Among the broken statues of Valladolid
there's one whose foot's still welded

to the granite plinth
from which, like us, it draws its strength.

From that, and from those few boiled beans.
We cannot gormandize upon

the flesh of Cain and Abel
without some melancholic vegetable

bringing us back to earth, to the boudoir
in the abattoir.

Our civil wars, the crumbling of empires,
the starry nights without number

safely under our belts,
have only slightly modified the tilt

of the acanthus leaf,
its spiky puce-and-alabaster an end in itself.

Capercaillies

In a deep, in a dark wood, somewhere north of Loch Lomond,
Saint Joan and I should be in our element;
the electroplated bracken and furze
have only gradually given way to pines and firs

in which a—what?—a straggler from Hadrian's
sixth legion squats over the latrine
and casts a die. His spurs suggest a renegade
Norman knight, as does his newly-prinked

escutcheon of sable on a field of sable,
whereas the hens—three, four, five—in fashionable
yellow gum-boots, are meekly back from Harrods.
Once a year (tonight, perhaps) such virtue has its reward;

raising his eyes to heaven—as if about to commit hara-
kiri—the cock will hop on each in turn and, unhurri-
edly, do three or four push-ups,
reaching all too soon for a scuffed Elizabeth Bishop.

'Paul? Was it you put the *pol* in polygamy
or was it somebody else?' While their flesh is notably gamey
even in bilberry-time, their winter tack's
mainly pine-shoots, so they now smack

of nothing so much as turpentine.
Room 233. Through a frosted, half-opened
window I listen to the love burps and borborygms of a capercaillie
('horse of the woods', the name means in Gaelic)

as he challenges me to mortal combat.

The following morning, Saint Joan has moved into the camp-bed.

Asra

The night I wrote your name in biro on my wrist
we would wake before dawn; back to back: duellists.

The Panther

For what it's worth, the last panther in Massachusetts
was brought to justice
in the woods beyond these meadows
and hung by its heels from a meat-hook
in what is now our kitchen.

(The house itself is something of a conundrum,
built as it was by an Ephraim Cowan from Antrim.)

I look in one evening while Jean
is jelly-making. She has rendered down pounds of grapes
and crab-apples
to a single jar
at once impenetrable and clear:
'Something's missing. This simply won't take.'

The air directly under the meat-hook—
it quakes, it quickens;
on a flagstone, the smudge of the tippy-tip of its nose.

The Briefcase

For Seamus Heaney

I held the briefcase at arm's length from me;
the oxblood or liver
eelskin with which it was covered
had suddenly grown supple.

I'd been waiting in line for the cross-town
bus when an almighty cloudburst
left the sidewalk a raging torrent.

And though it contained only the first
inkling of this poem, I knew I daren't
set the briefcase down
to slap my pockets for an obol—

for fear it might slink into a culvert
and strike out along the East River
for the sea. By which I mean the 'open' sea.

from **Madoc: A Mystery**

[THALES]

When he ventured forth from the smallroom
he activated a sensor-tile
that set off the first in a series of alarms
and sent a ripple through Unitel.

He was running now. A frog
scrawled across a lily-pond.
A kind of hopscotch frug.
There'd be a twenty second

delay. Then he'd almost certainly succumb
to their cotton-candy
scum-foam.
He'd only to whisper 'In Xanadu . . .'

and smile 'did Kubla Khan . . .'
His voice-count
was still good. Then a retina-scan.
On the stroke of three the door opened

and all hell broke loose.
There were Geckoes armed with Zens
to either side. He let go of his old valise.
And since

there was nowhere to turn
he turned to the unruffled, waist-deep hedge
with its furbelow of thorns
and deckle-edged

razor-ribbon.
One or two Geckoes began to applaud.
He took the plunge. Whereupon
he became just another twist in the plot.

[ANAXIMANDER]

'Are you telling me that South was as free as a bird
to wander through the Dome
and it wasn't until he went to take a dump . . .'
'Then we knew something untoward

had happened.' 'How?' 'He weighed more rather than less
when he left the crapper.'
'Much more?' 'Exactly as much as the scrap of paper
we repossessed from his valise.'

[PARMENIDES]

A woodchuck gets up on its hind legs and tail
to check the azimuth
and squinny
down the fork in the trail

where the Way of Seeming and the Way of Truth
diverge. He upsets
his own little tin pot and trivet
to tumble-pour

down the burrow
from which he derived.
September, 1798. What could be more apposite
than that into this vale

a young ass or hinny
bear Samuel Taylor Coleridge?
We see him reach
into his pantaloons for a small, sea-green vial,

then be overwhelmed by another pang of guilt.
A flock of siskins
or some such finches
blunders up from the Susquehanna.

Given the vagaries
and caracoles
of her star-gazing Narragansett colt
it's unlikely that Sara Fricker

will ever make good the yards, feet and inches
between herself and S.T.C. A grackle
blurts out from the choke-cherries.
The colt can no longer suppress a snicker.

[ANAXAGORAS]

—

For a week now, since he came down with a fever,
Cornplanter and Red Jacket

have kept a vigil by Handsome Lake.
Sassafras. Elder.

Ewe's-milk.
They look at each other. They speculate

on whether his chest might be colder.
They press a rust-speckled,

jagged
glass to his mouth. It refuses to mist over.

—

In the light of the X Y Z affair
America and France are limbering up for war.

—

Near Femme Osage creek, on the lower Missouri,
Daniel Boone

comes on a beaver caught in two separate
traps.

It has gnawed both drubs
to the bone.

This beaver, like the woodchuck, is an emissary
from the Great Spirit.

[SOCRATES]

—

While one by one the rest of the cavalcade
draw level
with her in the glade.
Her sisters, Edith Southey and Mary Lovell,

are astride a strawberry roan.
Their man-servant, Shad,
is driving a spanking-new, iron-
shod

wagon in which Lovell himself is laid.
Three days ago, a wood-sprite
worried his shoulder-blade.
The wound has begun to suppurate.

Messrs Allen, Burnett, Le Grice and Favell
dismount and pitch
the first of several
bell-tents. A pure-white spaniel bitch

runs rings round them. Cinnamond builds
a fire, helps Lovell to the shelter of a cairn
of stones and applies another poultice
of hemlock-bark and acorns.

—

A thrum of hooves. If Southey is to Bucephalus
as a flame is to its wick
then Southey is a flame.

He clutches a small, already-battered valise,
a sheaf of quills, a quire of vellum.
He cancels everything in his wake.

[ANTISTHENES]

Coleridge follows a white spaniel
through the caverns of the Domdaniel.

[EUCLID]

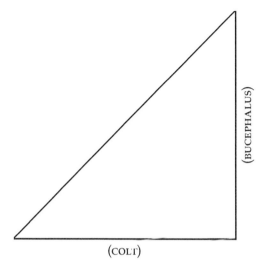

(BUCEPHALUS)

(COLT)

[PLOTINUS]

—

The next morning, before they pass under
the mare's tail of a waterfall

where the Way of Reason
narrows to the Way of Faith,

Coleridge and Southey must pause
to draw lots. They wave

to Shad and the rest of their tearful,
much-depleted garrison,

who'll try for Ulster at their own pace
before the onset of winter.

—

Shad waves back, and bends for the mattock
he'll use to dig

a grave for the dog
when it comes to him in a flash—MADOC.

[BENEDICT]

Southey takes its tongue between finger and thumb
and the door-bell is struck dumb, de dum.

[DUNS SCOTUS]

Southey has wedged himself between two boulders
by the side of a creek.
His pine-cone fire splutters
out. Bucephalus speaks to him in halting Greek:

'This is indeed a holy place
dedicated to the sun god, Bel.'
Southey can but dimly make out the blaze
on his poll:

'Were the secret of the ogam
script on the edge of this standing stone
known to the Reverend Samson Occom
he would hold it in disdain.

Yet his own people, the Mohegan,
are the seed of the Celtic chieftain, Eoghan.'

[OCCAM]

One or two things we should know about Joseph Brant.

He was born in 1743, the son of a ginseng-gatherer.

His name means 'two sticks tied together'.

In the spring of 1761 he received a good conduct medal from George the Third for his services against the French.

He studied Hebrew, Latin and Greek at Wheelock's Academy, now Dartmouth College.

In 1776 he visited London, where the King presented him with a Mason's apron. He was interviewed by James Boswell for *The London Magazine*.

He sided with the British during the Revolutionary War.

In 1797 he dined with Aaron Burr and his daughter, Theodosia, who considered serving him a human head.

Though he is nominally 'King of the Mohawks' he is plagued by schisms.

Five years ago his son, Isaac, tried to kill him.

This past winter a strangled white dog was slung from a pole just outside Brant's Town.

This is enough to be going on with.

[ERASMUS]

Twelve months ago they embarked, de dum, Te Deum,
on a merchantman out of Rotterdam

and were seen off from the Bristol quay
by a bemused citizenry

including Hucks and Cottle, their fellow-
Pantisocrats, who now dismissed the plan as folly.

They would anchor briefly in an Irish harbour
to take on board the usual raparees

and rapscallions;
cattle, pigs, sheep and, of course, the stallion.

[MORE]

—

It's a year to the day since Thomas Jefferson
tabled his first version

of 'the mould-board
of least resistance' for a plow

to the American
Philosophical Society.

—

A year, too, since the Unitedman, the MacGuffin,
paid a Dutch captain one hundred guilders

and took passage on a coffin-
ship from Westport.

MacGuffin has now changed his name to 'Smith'.
He is in the service of Aaron Burr.

—

Little does Jefferson know, as he saddles the Morgan
and slopes off down to Mulberry Row

and the less-than-smooth
furrow of his light-skinned Jocasta,

that 'Smith' overhears them link and uncouple.
Little does he think that the world is out of kilter.

[LUTHER]

I was haunted by evil spirits, of whose presence, though unseen, I was aware. At length an arm appeared through a half-opened door, or rather a long hand. I ran up and caught it. I pulled at it with desperate effort, dragged a sort of shapeless body into the room and trampled upon it, crying out the while for horror.

(Southey)

[PASCAL]

Jefferson is so beside himself with glee
that he finishes off a carafe

of his best Médoc;
his newly-modified polygraph

will automatically
follow hand-in-glove

his copper-plate 'whippoorwill'
or 'praise' or 'love':

will run parallel to the parallel
realm to which it is itself the only clue.

[SPINOZA]

Brother, I rise to return the thanks of this nation to our ancient friends—if any such we have—for their good wishes towards us in attempting to teach us your religion. Perhaps your religion may be peculiarly adapted to your condition. You say that you destroyed the Son of the Great Spirit. Perhaps this is the merited cause of all your troubles and misfortunes.

Brother, we pity you. We wish you to bear to our good friends our best wishes. Inform them that in compassion towards them we are willing to send them missionaries to teach them our religion, habits, and customs. Perhaps you think we are ignorant and uninformed. Go, then, and teach the whites. Select, for example, the people of Buffalo. Improve their morals and refine their habits. Make them less disposed to cheat Indians. Make the whites generally less inclined to make Indians drunk and to take from them their lands. Let us know the tree by the blossoms, and the blossoms by the fruit.

(Red Jacket)

[HOOKE]

O spirochete. O spirochete. O spirochete.

[ROUSSEAU]

December, 1802. The two Toms, Jefferson and Paine,
look out through the silver birches,
past undulating spruce and pine,
to the illimitabilities of the Louisiana Purchase.

74

[DIDEROT]

In the downstairs study, Jefferson's aide-de-camp
makes a tally of blankets, hats and gloves;
opium, laudanum,
cinnamon, oil of cloves;

marlinspikes, wimbles,
gimlets and awls;
needles and thimbles;
fish-hooks; powder and ball;

the theodolite, quadrant, compass and chain . . .
Except for his not as yet having got
to grips with the code

based on the key word 'artichokes',
all's set fair for his clandestine mission.
Meriwether Lewis swaggers up and out to the jakes.

[PUTNAM]

'Not until you see the whites of their eyes.'

[SMITH]

A small gust of wind through the open window.
A gasp on a cello or viola.
A flittering across the portfolio
Lewis has left untied.

A cursory glance
at the ledgers and log books.
Abracadabra. Hocus-pocus.
A thumb through a well-thumbed Linnaeus.

Until, among bills-of-lading and manifests
and almanacs and a Mercator
plan of the heavens,

this: the map drawn up by John Evans
that shows such a vast
unsulliedness the very candle gulps and gutters.

[PRIESTLEY]

—

On the western branch of the Susquehanna,
Putnam Catlin's

intent on guddling
a trout.

—

Only when she's in her last agony
does the trout renege

on a silver ear-ring
and cough it up and spit it out.

—

It lies on the floor of the birch-bark canoe.
Catlin's all of a sudden filled with dread.

[SAUSSURE]

—

August 7th. Lewis has sent a hunting-party
in search of the deserters, Moses Reed and La Liberté.

—

August 11th. The Captains mull
over the tumulus or mole

where the Omaha chief, Blackbird,
was buried

on his white war-horse.

—

August 18th. Reed's brought back and forced

to run a gauntlet of ramrods
and switches. Boils and buboes. Haemorrhoids.

—

August 20th. Floyd dies of colic and melancholia.

—

August 25th. His spirit clambers up the holy

Mound of the Little People, to the moans
of its thousands of eighteen-inch-high demons.

—

October 14th. John Newman is sentenced to seventy-five
lashes for having uttered a mutinous oath.

—

October 25th. Though the sandstone bluffs and spurs
give way, for the most part, to sparsely-

wooded, deeply-fissured mesas
redolent of wormwood, of the artemisia's

turpentine and camphor,
there's still the occasional, delicately-chamfered

column of honey- or salmon-coloured querns
surmounted, as here, by an obsidian cornice.

Camphor and turpentine. Elk-slots. Bear-scats.
Drouillard and Shields, the scouts,

can see directly across the stately saraband
of the Missouri to the corresponding

scumble of mosques and minarets
and the three-hundred-odd Mandans and Minnetarees.

[BENTHAM]

—

In fancy now, beneath the twilight gloom,
come, let me lead thee o'er this 'second Rome',
this embryo capital, where fancy sees
squares in morasses, obelisks in trees.

—

October, 1804. A secret letter from Merry to Burr
encloses these lines by Tom 'Little' Moore:

—

The patriot, fresh from Freedom's councils come,
now pleased retires to lash his slaves at home;
or woo, perhaps, some black Aspasia's charms,
and dream of freedom in his bondsmaid's arms.

—

Merry's seal is of ivory set in jade
and reads, predictably, IAƆ ꙄЯUOႱUOT.

[COOPER]

Strong evidence has been adduced that Madoc reached America, and
that his posterity exist there to this day, on the southern branches of
the Missouri, retaining their complexion, their language, and, in some
degree, their arts.

(Southey, Preface to *Madoc*, April 1805)

[FICHTE]

This very morning, a sixty-foot sloop
was seen to put in
at the Island. The dunt
of a light skiff

against the jetty.
While Aaron Burr
mesmerizes his host
with the barbel

of an Idea,
the ubiquitous 'Smith'
hovers about the pier.
He's absorbed by the dent

below his own water-line. A purple
tick-bite no bigger than a button.
Burr raises his glass to Blennerhassett:
'Syllabub. Syllabub. Syllabub.'

[SMITH]

Madoc is doing well; rather more than half the edition is sold, which is much for so heavy a volume. The sale, of course, will flag now, till the world shall have settled what they please to think of the poem. The Monthly *is all malice, and is beneath all notice; but look at the* Edinburgh, *and you will see that Jeffrey himself does not know what he is about. William Taylor has criticised it for the* Annual *very favourably and very ably. Taylor has said it is the best English poem that has left the press since* Paradise Lost; *indeed, this is not exaggerated praise, for, unfortunately, there is no competition.*

(Southey)

[SCHELLING]

September 5th, 1805

We assembled the Chiefs & warriers and Spoke to them with much difficuelty as what we Said had to pass through Several languages before it got into theirs, which is Spoken much thro the throught.

(Clark)

These natives have the Stranges language of any we have ever yet seen. They appear to us as though they had an Impedement in their Speech.

(Ordway)

80

These Savages has the Strangest language of any we have ever Seen.
They appear to us to have an Empediment in their Speech or bur on
their tongue. We take these Savages to be the Welch Indians if their be
any Such.

(Whitehouse)

[SCHOPENHAUER]

—

'And where did you come by the Nez Percé pony?'

—

Coleridge absentmindedly ties a knot
in the waist-cord of his breeks.

—

'Are you with the Northwest or X Y Companies?'

—

Retina. From the Latin *rete*, a net.

—

'When I struck the "c" from *castor*
I found myself in the company of John Jacob Astor.'

—

In the waist-cord of his breeks
he inextricably tightens the knot.

—

'Billet him with Newman in the red pirogue.'

[FARADAY]

'Tis said, in Summer's evening hour
Flashes the golden-colour'd flower
  A fair electric flame:
And so shall flash my love-charg'd eye
When all the heart's big ecstasy
  Shoots rapid through the frame.
                              (Coleridge)

[FEUERBACH]

—

The tinkle
of an Aeolian harp.

Eels.
Elvers.

An inkle
of black crêpe.

—

His pirogue
reels

through a sulphurous
brook.

—

What if Coleridge were to plait
a geyser's

cobalt-
azure

into a less than ideal
rope whereby

to wheedle-
warp

himself into the well, well, well
of his own fontanelle.

[FOUCAULT]

Even as Southey ponders the variables in torque
on the counter-weight and derrick

of the great ballista
he cannibalized

from that vividly-imagined
sky-machine's

wheels within wheels,
Bucephalus hints at the livid welts and weals

on his such-and-such:
'You're already under siege

from within, just as these blenny-blebs and blets
are storming my Bastille.'

[PEIRCE]

—

As the weeks have gone by, Coleridge feels less squeamish
when he finds a blue and yellow grub
in a raw bulb of quamash.

—

However long he maggots upon why the crop
of mangolds should suddenly spoil,
Southey is none the wiser.
He orders them plowed under. Goody-good for the soil.

—

Pike, pickerel. Hog, hoggerel.
Cock, cockerel. Dog, doggerel.

—

Beyond the ramparts, the False Face lifts his visor.

[EDISON]

—

Coleridge has fallen in with a band of Modocs
who extemporize a sudatory

from the overturned dory.
They ply him with such mild emetics

as yarrow and Oregon
grape. He's tantalized

84

by the all-pervasive tang of dulse
or caragreen.

—

That night the Modocs light a greasewood beacon
and repeatedly sound a conch.

—

The morning brings a party of Spokanes.
Their chief orders Coleridge the use of his wife

in exchange for (1) the kinnikinnick
and (2) the Sheffield knife.

[WHITEHEAD]

—

Southey wakes in a cold sweat;
penguins don't have white heads.

—

April, 1797

My dearest Cottle,
    I am fearful that Southey will begin to rely too much on story &
event *in his poems to the neglect of those* lofty imaginings *that are pe-
culiar to, & definitive of, the* POET.

(S.T. Coleridge)

[SCHILLER]

Hawk-nosed, with a hawk's clumsily seeled eye,
duodenum, de dum, de dum,
Cinnamond fastens the palfrey's reins
to his gelding's tail.

His wrinkled breeks
are of stuff you might take for shagreen.
He's breakfasted on an oatmeal bannock
or scone.

He tilts the whiskey bottle
at Shad, at the featureless, frank, smoked ham
of Shad's face. O for a flitch of salty
pork.

Nothing. Cinnamond coaxes the bung
into the bottle and yanks
at his loose-fitting, shalloon-lined galligaskins;
'Mon is the mezjur of all thungs.'

[JUNG]

—

Bear-claws; a soap-stone frog; two big-horn fleeces
sewn into their own rumens;

of all the totems, de dum, that might assuage
the Mandan gods, none will speak more eloquently

from the hogshead-shrine than this: this swatch
of a crimson mackinaw blanket.

—

Southey has now proscribed (1) the white dog ceremony
and (2) the society of False Faces.

[EINSTEIN]

December 11th, 1806. When the Wood County militia
led by Colonel Phelps
come at full gallop
across the Island, one breaks his neck, *eheu*,

on a ha-ha.
The jangle of a bayonet
across the spinet.
There's neither hide nor hair of Blennerhassett.

While his men slaughter and roast
a milch-
cow in the ruins

of the garden,
the Colonel pores over a rune
on the bog-oak lintel. Is it 'CROATAN' or 'CROATOAN'?

[BACHELARD]

Six hours ago, and twenty miles away, they had chanced
on a wagon drawn by a mule-team,
de dum,
and driven by a grizzly bear

who levelled his smooth-bore
not at them, but Shad,
and finished him off with a single shot.
He then stood his ground as, one by one, the Crows

charged at him in an elaborate criss-cross
only to cajole
him with their coup-crooks and cudgels.
When York swooped down and caught him by the scruff

of the neck, Cinnamond simply sloughed off
his skin and slithered
under the wagon like a lizard.
Then, as if this might indeed hold them at bay,

he lit a whisper of hay
and set fire to a semi-circle of sage-brush
that shortly engulfed the wagon, where he surely perished.
York's throat still rankles with aniseed.

[WITTGENSTEIN]

'Now your stumparumper is a connoisorrow who has lost his ras-
pectabilberry.'

[BENJAMIN]

Later that afternoon, or the next, a filibegged Byron will hobble
through the streets of Pisa
and trip over a cobble.
As he sprawls there, a group of boys
begin to jeer, '*Diavolo*'.
That night, he writes to Southey to propose
he either retract the 'Satanic' canard
or give him satisfaction. (This missive's intercepted by Kinnaird.)

[LEWIS]

Coleridge lays a comforting hand on Southey's shoulder.

[ADORNO]

—

April 19th, 1824. On the shore at Missolonghi
Byron's ball-and-chain is missing a link.

—

Independence Day, 1826. A gasp on a cello
or viola reverberates through Monticello.

The polygraph at its usual rigmarole.
The gopher pining for a caramel.

—

Jefferson clutches a bar of lye-soap
on which is scratched the name BEELZEBUB.

[GOODMAN]

*Now I am inclined to believe that the ten ships of Madoc, or Madawc,
made their way up the Mississippi and, at length, advanced up the
Missouri to the place where they have been known for many years
past by the name of the Mandans, a corruption or abbreviation, per-
haps, of 'Madawgwys', the name applied by the Welsh to the followers
of Madawc.*

(Catlin)

[BEAUVOIR]

'Where's my stumparumper? My confabulumper?
My maffrum? My goffrum? My swarnish pigglepow?'

[AUSTIN]

Even though the tree-girt auditorium,
de dum,

is deserted but for a troop
of nymphs and gnomes

and nixies,
Southey hikes up his tabard

and mounts the podium,
de dum.

As he warms to a diatribe
against his enemies

he nags
at the filigreed scabbard

of his sword
so as to emmmmmmmmmmmmphasize his words.

[CAMUS]

June 16th, 1837. The Mandan villages are ravaged by smallpox.

[GRICE]

November 16th. The last word on Edith Southey's lips is 'sentiment'.

[BARTHES]

March 20th, 1843. An almost naked 'Mandan' in harlequin
red and black lozenges
manages only one shot from his squirrel-gun
before a raiding-party of 'Shoshones'

rush his buffalo-wallow
and wrestle
him to the ground. His ululations are to no avail.
They take his scalp. The rehearsal

ends with the 'Shoshone' chief returning the pony-tail
wig to his victim
who stuffs it into a buckskin medicine-bundle,
his *vade mecum*,

which is then lodged in a glory-hole
back in his caravan.
This afternoon finds 'Catlin's Indian Gallery'
somewhere in deepest Wales. In the port, say, of Carnarvon.

[DERRIDA]

—

A glance back to the great palladium,
de dum,

as it goes up in flames.
Its voluminous

tulles and smoke-taffetas.
The fetid

stink of new-fangled creosote.
Tar-water. Tar-water and a sooty crust.

—

'At any moment now, the retina
will be in smithereens.'

—

The buckler affixed to the mast-head by a cleat
bears this device: a pair of gryphons

on a field of gold;
a scroll emblazoned with the word 'CROTONA'.

[HARMAN]

'Not "CROATAN", not "CROATOAN", but "CROTONA".'

[NOZICK]

—

May, 1843. 'Catlin's Indian Gallery' has now reached Ireland. Half-way between Belfast and Dublin, near the present site of Unitel West, the medicine-bag is either misplaced or stolen.

—

May, 1846. President Polk engages a secret agent against Mexico. His name? 'Magoffin'.

—

May, 1873. The Modocs, led by Captain Jack, are systematically
hunted down on the laver-breads of Oregon.

[KRISTEVA]

'Signifump. Signifump. Signifump.'

[HAWKING]

—

The Cayugas have shouldered their Lasabers
and smoothed their scalp-locks.

A scrap of paper in a valise
now falls within the range

of a sensor-tile. The corridor
awash in slime. Trifoliate Chinese orange.

One leg held on by a frivolous
blood-garter.

—

It will all be over, de dum,
in next to no time–

long before 'The fluted cypresses
rear'd up their living obelisks'

has sent a shiver, de dum, de dum,
through Unitel, its iridescent Dome.

Incantata

In memory of Mary Farl Powers

I thought of you tonight, *a leanbh*, lying there in your long barrow
colder and dumber than a fish by Francisco de Herrera,
as I X-Actoed from a spud the Inca
glyph for a mouth: thought of that first time I saw your pink
spotted torso, distant-near as a nautilus,
when you undid your portfolio, yes indeedy,
and held the print of what looked like a cankered potato
at arm's length—your arms being longer, it seemed, than Lugh's.

Even Lugh of the Long (sometimes the Silver) Arm
would have wanted some distance between himself and the army-
    worms
that so clouded the sky over St Cloud you'd have to seal
the doors and windows and steel
yourself against their nightmarish *déjeuner sur l'herbe*:
try as you might to run a foil
across their tracks, it was to no avail;
the army-worms shinnied down the stove-pipe on an army-worm rope.

I can hardly believe that, when we met, my idea of 'R and R'
was to get smashed, almost every night, on sickly-sweet Demarara
rum and Coke: as well as leaving you a grass widow
(remember how Krapp looks up 'viduity'?),
after eight or ten or twelve of those dark rums
it might be eight or ten or twelve o'clock before I'd land
back home in Landseer Street, deaf and blind
to the fact that not only was I all at sea, but in the doldrums.

Again and again you'd hold forth on your own version of Thomism,
your own *Summa*
Theologiae that in everything there is an order,
that the things of the world sing out in a great oratorio:
it was Thomism, though, tempered by *La Nausée*,
by His Nibs Sam Bethicket,
and by that Dublin thing, that an artist must walk down Baggott
Street wearing a hair-shirt under the shirt of Nessus.

'*D'éirigh me ar maidin*,' I sang, '*a tharraingt chun aoinigh mhóir*':
our first night, you just had to let slip that your secret amour
for a friend of mine was such
that you'd ended up lying with him in a ditch
under a bit of whin, or gorse, or furze,
somewhere on the border of Leitrim, perhaps, or Roscommon:
'gamine,' I wanted to say, 'kimono';
even then it was clear I'd never be at the centre of your universe.

Nor should I have been, since you were there already, your own *Ding*
an sich, no less likely to take wing
than the Christ you drew for a Christmas card as a pupa
in swaddling clothes: and how resolutely you would pooh-pooh
the idea I shared with Vladimir and Estragon,
with whom I'd been having a couple of jars,
that this image of the Christ-child swaddled and laid in the manger
could be traced directly to those army-worm dragoons.

I thought of the night Vladimir was explaining to all and sundry
the difference between *geantrai* and *suantrai*
and you remarked on how you used to have a crush
on Burt Lancaster as Elmer Gantry, and Vladimir went to brush
the ash off his sleeve with a legerdemain
that meant only one thing—'Why does he put up with this crap?'—
and you weighed in with 'To live in a dustbin, eating scrap,
seemed to Nagg and Nell a most eminent domain.'

How little you were exercised by those tiresome literary intrigues,
how you argued me to have no more truck
than the Thane of Calder
with a fourth estate that professes itself to be *'égalitaire'*
but wants only blood on the sand: yet, irony of ironies,
you were the one who, in the end,
got yourself up as a *retiarius* and, armed with net and trident,
marched from Mount Street to the Merrion Square arena.

In the end, you were the one who went forth to beard the lion,
you who took the DART line
every day from Jane's flat in Dun Laoghaire, or Dalkey,
dreaming your dream that the subterranean Dodder and Tolka
might again be heard above the *hoi polloi*
for whom Irish 'art' means a High Cross at Carndonagh or Corofin
and *The Book of Kells*: not until the lion cried craven
would the poor Tolka and the poor Dodder again sing out for joy.

I saw you again tonight, in your jump-suit, thin as a rake,
your hand moving in such a deliberate arc
as you ground a lithographic stone
that your hand and the stone blurred to one
and your face blurred into the face of your mother, Betty Wahl,
who took your failing, ink-stained hand
in her failing, ink-stained hand
and together you ground down that stone by sheer force of will.

I remember your pooh-poohing, as we sat there on the *Enterprise*,
my theory that if your name is Powers
you grow into it or, at least,
are less inclined to tremble before the likes of this bomb-blast
further up the track: I myself was shaking like a leaf
as we wondered whether the I.R.A. or the Red
Hand Commandos or even the Red
Brigades had brought us to a standstill worthy of Hamm and Clov.

Hamm and Clov; Nagg and Nell; Watt and Knott;
the fact is that we'd been at a standstill long before the night
things came to a head,
long before we'd sat for half the day in the sweltering heat
somewhere just south of Killnasaggart
and I let slip a name—her name—off my tongue
and you turned away (I see it now) the better to deliver the sting
in your own tail, to let slip your own little secret.

I thought of you again tonight, thin as a rake, as you bent
over the copper plate of 'Emblements',
its tidal wave of army-worms into which you all but disappeared:
I wanted to catch something of its spirit
and yours, to body out your disembodied *vox*
clamantis in deserto, to let this all-too-cumbersome device
of a potato-mouth in a potato-face
speak out, unencumbered, from its long, low, mould-filled box.

I wanted it to speak to what seems always true of the truly great,
that you had a winningly inaccurate
sense of your own worth, that you would second-guess
yourself too readily by far, that you would rally to any cause
before your own, mine even,
though you detected in me a tendency to put
on too much artificiality, both as man and poet,
which is why you called me 'Polyester' or 'Polyurethane'.

The last time in Dublin, I copied with a quill dipped in oak-gall
onto a sheet of vellum, or maybe a human caul,
a poem for *The Great Book of Ireland*: as I watched the low
swoop over the lawn today of a swallow
I thought of your animated talk of Camille Pissarro
and André Derain's *The Turning Road, L'Estaque*:
when I saw in that swallow's nest a face in a mud-pack
from that muddy road I was filled again with a profound sorrow.

You must have known already, as we moved from the 'Hurly Burly'
to McDaid's or Riley's,
that something was amiss: I think you even mentioned a homeopath
as you showed off the great new acid-bath
in the Graphic Studio, and again undid your portfolio
to lay out your latest works; I try to imagine the strain
you must have been under, pretending to be as right as rain
while hearing the bells of a church from some long-flooded valley.

From the Quabbin reservoir, maybe, where the banks and bakeries
of a dozen little submerged Pompeii reliquaries
still do a roaring trade: as clearly as I saw your death-mask
in that swallow's nest, you must have heard the music
rise from the muddy ground between
your breasts as a nocturne, maybe, by John Field;
to think that you thought yourself so invulnerable, so inviolate,
that a little cancer could be beaten.

You must have known, as we walked through the ankle-deep clabber
with Katherine and Jean and the long-winded Quintus Calaber,
that cancer had already made such a breach
that you would almost surely perish:
you must have thought, as we walked through the woods
along the edge of the Quabbin,
that rather than let some doctor cut you open
you'd rely on infusions of hardock, hemlock, all the idle weeds.

I thought again of how art may be made, as it was by André Derain,
of nothing more than a turn
in the road where a swallow dips into the mire
or plucks a strand of bloody wool from a strand of barbed wire
in the aftermath of Chickamauga or Culloden
and build from pain, from misery, from a deep-seated hurt,
a monument to the human heart
that shines like a golden dome among roofs rain-glazed and leaden.

I wanted the mouth in this potato-cut
to be heard far beyond the leaden, rain-glazed roofs of Quito,
to be heard all the way from the southern hemisphere
to Clontarf or Clondalkin, to wherever your sweet-severe
spirit might still find a toe-hold
in this world: it struck me then how you would be aghast
at the thought of my thinking you were some kind of ghost
who might still roam the earth in search of an earthly delight.

You'd be aghast at the idea of your spirit hanging over this vale
of tears like a jump-suited jump-jet whose vapour-trail
unravels a sky: for there's nothing, you'd say, nothing over
and above the sky itself, nothing but cloud-cover
reflected in a thousand lakes; it seems that Minne-
sota itself means 'sky-tinted water', that the sky is a great slab
of granite or iron ore that might at any moment slip
back into the worked-out sky-quarry, into the worked-out sky-mines.

To use the word 'might' is to betray you once too often, to betray
your notion that nothing's random, nothing arbitrary:
the gelignite weeps, the hands fly by on the alarm clock,
the '*Enterprise*' goes clackety-clack
as they all must; even the car hijacked that morning in the Cross,
that was preordained, its owner spread on the bonnet
before being gagged and bound or bound
and gagged, that was fixed like the stars in the Southern Cross.

The fact that you were determined to cut yourself off in your prime
because it was *pre*-determined has my eyes abrim:
I crouch with Belacqua
and Lucky and Pozzo in the Acacacac-
ademy of Anthropopopometry, trying to make sense of the '*quaquaqua*'
of that potato-mouth; that mouth as prim
and proper as it's full of self-opprobrium,
with its '*quaquaqua*', with its 'Quoiquoiquoiquoiquoiquoiquoiq'.

That's all that's left of the voice of Enrico Caruso
from all that's left of an opera-house somewhere in Matto Grosso,
all that's left of the hogweed and horehound and cuckoo-pint,
of the eighteen soldiers dead at Warrenpoint,
of the Black Church clique and the Graphic Studio claque,
of the many moons of glasses on a tray,
of the brewery-carts drawn by moon-booted drays,
of those jump-suits worn under your bottle-green worsted cloak.

Of the great big dishes of chicken lo mein and beef chow mein,
of what's mine is yours and what's yours mine,
of the oxlips and cowslips
on the banks of the Liffey at Leixlip
where the salmon breaks through the either/or neither/nor nether
reaches despite the temple-veil
of itself being rent and the penny left out overnight on the rail
is a sheet of copper when the mail-train has passed over.

Of the bride carried over the threshold, hey, only to alight
on the limestone slab of another threshold,
of the swarm, the cast,
the colt, the spew of bees hanging like a bottle of Lucozade
from a branch the groom must sever,
of Emily Post's ruling, in *Etiquette*,
on how best to deal with the butler being in cahoots
with the cook when they're both in cahoots with the chauffeur.

Of that poplar-flanked stretch of road between Leiden
and The Hague, of the road between Rathmullen and Ramelton,
where we looked so long and hard
for some trace of Spinoza or Amelia Earhart,
both of them going down with their engines on fire:
of the stretch of road somewhere near Urney
where Orpheus was again overwhelmed by that urge to turn
back and lost not only Eurydice but his steel-strung lyre.

Of the sparrows and finches in their bell of suet,
of the bitter-sweet
bottle of Calvados we felt obliged to open
somewhere near Falaise, so as to toast our new-found *copains*,
of the priest of the parish
who came enquiring about our 'status', of the hedge-clippers
I somehow had to hand, of him running like the clappers
up Landseer Street, of my subsequent self-reproach.

Of the remnants of Airey Neave, of the remnants of Mountbatten,
of the famous *andouilles*, of the famous *boudins*
noirs et blancs, of the barrel-vault
of the Cathedral at Rouen, of the flashlight, fat and roll of felt
on each of their sledges, of the music
of Joseph Beuys's pack of huskies, of that baldy little bugger
mushing them all the way from Berncastel through Bacarrat
to Belfast, his head stuck with honey and gold-leaf like a mosque.

Of Benjamin Britten's *Lachrymae*, with its gut-wrenching viola,
of Vivaldi's *Four Seasons*, of Frankie Valli's,
of Braque's great painting *The Shower of Rain*,
of the fizzy, lemon or sherbet-green *Rana*
temporaria plonked down in Trinity like a little Naugahyde pouffe,
of eighteen soldiers dead in Oriel,
of the weakness for a little fol-de-rol-de-rolly
suggested by the gap between the front teeth of the Wife of Bath.

Of *A Sunday Afternoon on the Island of La Grande Jatte,* of Seurat's
piling of tesserae upon tesserae
to give us a monkey arching its back
and the smoke arching out from a smoke-stack,
of Sunday afternoons in the Botanic Gardens, going with the flow
of the burghers of Sandy Row and Donegal
Pass and Andersonstown and Rathcoole,
of the army Landrover flaunt-flouncing by with its heavy furbelow.

Of Marlborough Park, of Notting Hill, of the Fitzroy Avenue
immortalized by Van 'His real name's Ivan'
Morrison, 'and him the dead spit
of Padraic Fiacc', of John Hewitt, the famous expat,
in whose memory they offer every year six of their best milch cows,
of the Bard of Ballymacarrett,
of every ungodly poet in his or her godly garret,
of Medhbh and Michael and Frank and Ciaran and 'wee' John
    Qughes.

Of the Belfast school, so called, of the school of hard knocks,
of your fervent eschewal of stockings and socks
as you set out to hunt down your foes
as implacably as the *tóraidheacht* through the Fews
of Redmond O'Hanlon, of how that 'd' and that 'c' aspirate
in *tóraidheacht* make it sound like a last gasp in an oxygen-tent,
of your refusal to open a vent
but to breathe in spirit of salt, the mordant salt-spirit.

Of how mordantly hydrochloric acid must have scored and scarred,
of the claim that boiled skirrets
can cure the spitting of blood, of that dank
flat somewhere off Morehampton Road, of the unbelievable stink
of valerian or feverfew simmering over a low heat,
of your sitting there, pale and gaunt,
with that great prescriber of boiled skirrets, Dr John Arbuthnot,
your face in a bowl of feverfew, a towel over your head.

Of the great roll of paper like a bolt of cloth
running out again and again like a road at the edge of a cliff,
of how you called a Red Admiral a Red
Admirable, of how you were never in the red
on either the first or the last
of the month, of your habit of loosing the drawstring of your purse
and finding one scrunched-up, obstreperous
note and smoothing it out and holding it up, pristine and pellucid.

Of how you spent your whole life with your back to the wall,
of your generosity when all the while
you yourself lived from hand
to mouth, of Joseph Beuys's pack of hounds
crying out from their felt and fat 'Atone, atone, atone',
of Watt remembering the '*Krak*! *Krek*! *Krik*!'
of those three frogs' karaoke
like the still, sad, *basso continuo* of the great quotidian.

Of a ground bass of sadness, yes, but also a sennet of hautboys
as the fat and felt hounds of Beuys O'Beuys
bayed at the moon over a caravan
in Dunmore East, I'm pretty sure it was, or Dungarvan:
of my guest appearance in your self-portrait not as a hidalgo
from a long line
of hidalgos but a hound-dog, a *leanbh*,
a dog that skulks in the background, a dog that skulks and stalks.

Of that self-portrait, of the self-portraits by Rembrandt van Rijn,
of all that's revelation, all that's rune,
of all that's composed, all composed of odds and ends,
of that daft urge to make amends
when it's far too late, too late even to make sense of the clutter
of false trails and reversed horseshoe tracks
and the aniseed we took it in turn to drag
across each other's scents, when only a fish is dumber and colder.

Of your avoidance of canned goods, in the main,
on account of the exceeeeeeeeeeeeeeeedingly high risk of ptomaine,
of corned beef in particular being full of crap,
of your delight, so, in eating a banana as ceremoniously as Krapp
but flinging the skin over your shoulder like a thrush
flinging off a shell from which it's only just managed to disinter
a snail, like a stone-faced, twelfth-century
FitzKrapp eating his banana by the mellow, yellow light of a rush.

Of the 'Yes, let's go' spoken by Monsieur Tarragon,
of the early ripening jargonelle, the tumorous jardon, the jargon
of jays, the jars
of tomato relish and the jars
of Victoria plums, absolutely *de rigueur* for a passable plum baba,
of the drawers full of balls of twine and butcher's string,
of Dire straits playing 'The Sultans of Swing,'
of the horse's hock suddenly erupting in those boils and buboes.

Of the Greek figurine of a pig, of the pig on a terracotta frieze,
of the sow dropping dead from some mysterious virus,
of your predilection for gammon
served with a sauce of coriander or cumin,
of the slippery elm, of the hornbeam or witch-, or even wych-,
hazel that's good for stopping a haemor-
rhage in mid-flow, of the merest of mere
hints of elderberry curing everything from sciatica to a stitch.

Of the decree *condemnator*, the decree *absolvitor*, the decree *nisi*,
of *Aosdána*, of *an chraobh cnuais*,
of the fields of buckwheat
taken over by garget, inkberry, scoke—all names for pokeweed—
of *Mother Courage*, of *Arturo Ui*,
of those Sunday mornings spent picking at sesame
noodles and all sorts and conditions of dim sum,
of tea and ham sandwiches in the Nesbitt Arms hotel in Ardara.

Of the day your father came to call, of your leaving your sick-room
in what can only have been a state of delirium,
of how you simply wouldn't relent
from your vision of a blind
watch-maker, of your fatal belief that fate
governs everything from the honey-rust of your father's terrier's
eyebrows to the horse that rusts and rears
in the furrow, of the furrows from which we can no more deviate

than they can from themselves, no more than the map of Europe
can be redrawn, than that Hermes might make a harp from his
    harpe,
than that we must live in a vale
of tears on the banks of the Lagan or the Foyle,
than that what we have is a done deal,
than that the Irish Hermes,
Lugh, might have leafed through his vast herbarium
for the leaf that had it within it, Mary, to anoint and anneal,

than that Lugh of the Long Arm might have found in the midst of
    lus
na leac or *lus na treatha* or *Frannc-lus,*
in the midst of eyebright, or speedwell, or tansy, an antidote,
than that this *Incantata*
might have you look up from your plate of copper or zinc
on which you've etched the row upon row
of army-worms, than that you might reach out, arrah,
and take in your ink-stained hands my own hands stained with ink.

from Yarrow

Little by little it dawned on us that the row
of kale would shortly be overwhelmed by these pink
and cream blooms, that all of us

would be overwhelmed, that even if my da
were to lose an arm
or a leg to the fly-wheel

of a combine and be laid out on a tarp
in a pool of blood and oil
and my ma were to make one of her increasingly rare

appeals to some higher power, some *Deo*
this or that, all would be swept away by the stream
that fanned across the land.

—

All would be swept away: the altar where Montezuma's
daughter severed her own aorta
with an obsidian knife; where the young Ignatius

of Loyola knelt and, raising the visor of his bucket,
pledged himself either *Ad Major*
or *Ad Majorem Dei Gloriam*, I can't quite remember which.

—

For all would be swept away: the barn where the Pharaohs
had buried Tutankhamen;
where Aladdin found the magic lamp and ring;

where Ali Baba
watched the slave, Morgiana,
pour boiling oil on the thieves in their jars;

where Cicero smooth-talked the senators;
where I myself was caught up in the rush
of peers and paladins who ventured out with Charlemagne.

—

All would be swept away, all sold for scrap:
the hen-house improvised from a high-sided cattle-truck,
the coils of barbed wire, the coulter

of a plough, the pair of angle-iron
posts between which she'll waver, one day towards the end,
as she pins the clothes on the clothes-line.

—

For the moment, though, she thumbs through a seed-catalogue
she's borrowed from Tohill's of the Moy
while, quiet, almost craven,

he studies the grain in the shaft of a rake:
there are two palm-prints in blue stone
on the bib of his overalls

where he's absentmindedly put his hands
to his heart; in a den in St John's, Newfoundland, I browse
on a sprig of *Achillea millefolium*, as it's classed.

—

Achillea millefolium: with its bedraggled, feathery leaf
and pink (less red
than mauve) or off-white flower, its tight little knot

of a head,
it's like something keeping a secret
from itself, something on the tip of its own tongue.

—

Would that I might take a comfort in the vestigial scent
of a yarrow-sprig, a yarrow-spurt
I've plucked from the somewhat unorthodox

funerary vase
that fills one grate:
from the other there's a chortle of methane-gas

(is it methane
that's so redolent of the apple-butt?)
through a snow-capped sierra of non-combustible coal.

—

Would that I might as readily follow
this nosegay of yarrow as Don Junipero Serra
led us all the way back

along *El Camino Real*
by the helter-skelter path
of poppies we'd sown in the sap-sweet April rain.

—

I zap the remote control: that same poor elk or eland
dragged down by a bobolink;
a Spanish *Lear*; the umpteenth *Broken Arrow*;

a boxing-match; Robert Hughes dismantling Dada;
a Michael Jackson video
in which our friends, the Sioux, will peel

the face off a white man whose metacarp-
al bones, with those of either talus,
they've already numbered; the atmosphere's so rare

that if Michael's moon-suit of aluminium foil
were suddenly to split at the seams
he'd not only buy, but fertilize, the farm.

—

I crouch with Jim in the apple-butt on the *Marie Celeste*
while my half-eaten pomeroy
shows me its teeth: a fine layer of talc

has bandaged my hands;
it's Mexico, 1918;
this arm belongs to the pugilist-poet, Arthur Cravan;

it's enshrined now on the wall
of the den between a plaster of Paris
cow's skull and a stuffed ortolan, or Carolina crake.

—

It's Mexico, 1918, and I'm leaning out over the strake
with the inconsolable Myrna Loy,
whose poet-pugilist's

yawl
has almost certainly sunk like a stone:
'*J'y avais trouvé une combinaison idéal et idyllique—*

mon Artilutteur Ecrivain';
the label on the rake reads 'Pierce';
I'm thinking of those who have died by their own hands.

—

All I remember was a reprieve from *'seachain droch-chómhluadar'*
as she last rinsed my hair: she'd sung 'Eileen Aroon'

or some such ditty and scrubbed and scrubbed
till the sink was full of dreck;
'Stay well away from those louts and layabouts at the loanin'-end.'

—

Was it not now time, they urged, to levy the weregild, the *éiric*,
on the seed and breed of that scum-bag, Mountjoy,
that semioticonoclast

who took it upon himself to smash Shane O'Neill's
coronation-stone
on the chalky slopes of Tullahogue?

Was it not now time for the Irish to break the graven
image of a Queen whose very blotting-paper
was black, black with so much blood on her hands?

—

Like a little green heron, or 'fly-up-the-creek',
I flap above Carrickmore and Pomeroy
with volume one of Burton's translation of *The Lusiads*:

'One for all,'
I hear a cry go up, 'and all for one,'
followed by *'S'é tuar oilc*

an t-éan sin, agus leabhar in a chroibhín';
that was the year I did battle with Sir Bors
for Iseult the Fair (not Iseult of the White Hands).

—

Now I took the little awl I'd used with such consummate skill
to scuttle *The Golden Vanitee*
and picked the locks

on the old suitcase
in which was hidden the two-page spread
from *The News of the World*: after stopping by the cattle-grid

to pick up Laudine and Yvain
I smiled as I thought of the awl (was it a brace and bit?)
wrapped in a photo of Mandy Rice Davies.

—

The two-tone Cadillac's engine-block was a vice
lapped in a coil
of barbed wire and wedged between an apple-box

and a packing-crate:
as I crossed the bridge, I was so intent
on Freedom's green slip and Freedom's green sprout

her '*Ná bac leis an craoibhín aoibhinn*'
and 'Stay clear of those louts and layabouts'
were quite lost on me; I promptly stepped on the gas.

—

'O come ye back,' I heard her sing, 'O come ye back
to Erin':
I was somewhat more exercised by the fact that my yourali

supply was running so low
I might well have to spend my last cruzeiro
on an ounce of civet, or resort to my precious *Bufo bufo*.

—

The magical toad entrusted to me by Francisco Pizarro
might still be good against this bird that continued to prink
itself, alas,

even as we left Sitanda's
kraal and struck out, God between us and all harm,
for the deep north: that was the year Jack McCall would deal

the dead man's hand to Earp,
the year Captain Good was obliged to shave in inco-oil
and S—— got hooked on 'curare';

the year Scragga and Infandoos
joined Quatermain in reciting 'The Jackdaw of Rheims'
as we plunged deeper into Kukuanaland.

—

Only yesterday, as I shlepped out to Newark on the PATH
whom should I spot but two Japanese guys wearing fanny-packs:
I recognized them as 'Basho' and 'Sora'

from Avenue A; I knew by the tags on their mule-train
that they were just getting back from the Lowlands Low;
'Tooralooraloora,' Basho gave me a stupid grin, 'tooralooralay.'

—

'Tirra lirra,' S—— sang when we were stopped by the 'fuzz'
as she drove back to school:
she was reading, it seemed, as deeply into Maalox

as Malebranche, Rennies as René Descartes:
I helped her move into a 'pad', as she styled her apartment,
in which Herrick's *Hesperides* and a can of Sprite

and Duchamp's 'The Bride Stripped Bare by Her Bachelors, Even'
all said one thing—'I masturbate';
she was writing now on *Ulster: From C.S. Lewis to C.S. Gas.*

—

'Tirra lirra lirra,' was what she sang to Umslopogaas
and myself to, like, break the ice
when we first went to see her in detox:

an albino ginko, or some such sport;
she was now deeply into Lloyd Cole
and Julio Cortázar and, *Dios me libre*, Fuentes;

Lloyd 'King' Cole, she'd dubbed him; Warren Zevon;
as for U2's Edge, his 'Bad'
put him up there with Jimi and Eric, a 'Guitar Great'.

—

Five days north of Sitanda's kraal we were joined by Sigurd,
his twin cousins, Hrut and Knut,
and Lieutenant Henry Ark, also known as Eric the Red:

it was Eric who cut us each a strip of biltong
from the shield carried by his son, Leif;
Leif Ericson's shield was covered with chlordiazepoxide.

—

'How dare you,' began Milady Clarik, 'how dare you desecrate
the memory of Connolly and Clarke and Ceannt':
she brandished *The Little Red*

Book of Mao Tse-Tung;
'How dare you blather on about the Caliph
of Baghdad when you should strike while the iron's hot.'

—

'Surely,' S—— chimed in, 'surely the time is at hand
for the Hatfields and McCoys
to recognize their common bond?' (It was Milady *Clark*

who'd given her a copy of Ian Adamson's *The Cruthin*,
of which she'd bought a thousand tonnes
for 'intellectual ballast'.)

Together they'd entered into dialogue
with the first mate of a ship registered in Valparaiso
who had 'connections' in the Transvaal.

—

Ben Gunn would now gladly have red-hewed his right hand
for a piece of mouse-trap cheese, when the fairy Terdelaschoye
rustled up some *Caprice des Dieux*: so it was that Erec

and Enid and I hoisted the main-sail (complete with raven)
and hung the lodestone
by an elast-

ic band; *Caprice*, for Land's sake, from the 'goat-like'
caprioles and capers
of those Athenian galleys with their tu-whit-tutelary owls.

—   '

Only moments later, I was bending over to tie a slip-
knot when I looked up suddenly and the rough tree rail
had been superseded by the coast

of Africa; it struck me then that the limpet-mine
in the *Hispaniola's* hold
had been planted there by the pesky Pedro Navarro.

—

That must have been from our last trip up the Guadalquivir:
we'd given the Athenian galleys the slip
and put in at Seville rather than try to hold

our course for Dover, its cliffs *chomh bán le haol*,
with our cargo of calomel (or calamine);
the Guadalquivir had been our Rubicon; the die was cast.

—

To make matters worse, Ben reported that he'd just heard
the unmistakable tu-whit
tu-whoo of the *gubernaculum* in the stern

of a Roman galley. We were getting ready to open
fire
on anything that moved when *'Vamos, muchachos, vamos a ver'*

came out of nowhere, followed by a barge
with a triangular sail—a jib, to be precise—cut
from a single piece of lateen.

—

From the cut of their jib we took the crew for a horde
of Cruthin dyed with woad:
it hadn't occurred to us that we ourselves might turn

blue after a month in an open
boat; it transpired
these legionnaires had been set adrift by Septimius Severus

in 211 A.D.; we shared what was left of our porridge,
then joined them in a game of quoits
on the deck of the *Caledonia*.

—

Who should hove into view, with a boy-troop from St Enda's,
but Pearse himself: together with the gallioteers,
we went ashore and began the long trek

north from St Enda's kraal; when the tree-line
gave way to unfamiliar scrub
we knew we'd rounded not the Cape of Good Hope but Cape Horn.

—

That was the year Mike Fink was a bouncer at 'The Bitter End'
on Bleecker Street: 'The times are out of kilter,'
he marked to S——, eyeing the needle-tracks

on her arms; that was the year she would mainline
so much 'curare' they ran up two flags over her wing at Scripps.
(By 'curare', or 'yourali', she meant heroin.)

—

In view of these square red flags with square black centres
we turned back and fell to right away to gammon
the bow-spirit with baobab-

ropes and secure the cat's head and the catharping
against the impending hurricane:
we'd already stowed the sails (fore-, mizzen- and main-)

and breamed the hull with burning furze
and touched up the figurehead—an angel carved by William Rush
from the sturdiest of mahoganies, the Australian jarrah.

—

In a conventional tornada, the strains of her *'Che sera, sera'*
or 'The Harp That Once' would transport me back
to a bath resplendent with yarrow

(it's really a sink set on breeze- or cinder-blocks):
then I might be delivered
from the rail's monotonous 'alack, alack';

in a conventional envoy, her voice would be ever
soft, gentle and low
and the chrism of milfoil might over-

flow
as the great wheel
came full circle; here a bittern's bibulous *'Orinochone O'*

is counterpointed only by that corncrake, by the gulder-gowl
of a nightjar, I guess, above the open-cast mines,
by a quail's

indecipherable code; of the great cog-wheel, all that remains
is a rush of air—a wing-beat,
more like—past my head; even as I try to regain

my equilibrium, there's no more relief, no more respite
than when I scurried, click, down McParland's lane
with my arms crossed, click, under my armpits;

—

I can no more read between the lines
of the quail's 'Wet-my-lips' or his 'Quick, quick'
than get to grips with Friedrich Hölderlin

or that phrase in Vallejo having to do with the 'ache'
in his forearms; on the freshly-laid asphalt
a freshly-peeled willow-switch, or baton, shows a vivid mosaic

of gold on a black field, while over the fields
of buckwheat it's harder and harder to pin down a gowk's
poopookarian *ignis fatuus*;

though it slips, the great cog,
there's something about the quail's 'Wet-my-foot'
and the sink full of hart's-tongue, borage and common kedlock

that I've either forgotten or disavowed;
it has to do with a trireme, laden with ravensara,
that was lost with all hands between Ireland and Montevideo.

from The Prince of the Quotidian

The more I think of it, the more I've come to love
the tidal marshes of Hackensack,
the planes stacked
over Newark, even the smell of cloves

and chloroform
that sweetens Elizabeth.
(At Exit 9, the man in the toll-booth
almost lost an arm

to Oscar Mac Oscar, as we call the hound ...)
The more I think of it, the less I'm clear
as to why U2 should spend a year
remaking themselves as a garage band.

Which reminds me; we must see the new Wim Wenders.
In the meantime, let's rent *Pathfinder*.

—

Not for nothing would I versify
'The Alchemist and Barrister', rhyme (*pace* Longley) 'cat'
with 'dog', expand on the forsythia
that graces our back door : 'humdrum', 'inadequate',

'inconsequential journalese', 'a klieg light
masquerading as the moon'; none will,
I trust, look for a pattern in this crazy quilt
where all is random , 'all so trivial',

unless it be Erasmus, unless
Erasmus again steel
himself as his viscera are cranked out by a windlass

yard upon 'xanthous' yard;
again to steel himself, then somehow to exhort
the windlass-men to even greater zeal.

—

Much as I'm taken by Barry Douglas playing Rachmaninov
with the Ulster Orchestra
I remember why I've had enough
of the casuistry

by which pianists and painters and poets are proof
that all's not rotten in the state:
amid the cheers and cries of 'Bravo'
I hear the howls of seven dead

at a crossroads between Omagh and long Cookstown.
The 'trivial' happens where 'three roads' meet.
Does Saint Augustine

'trivialise' the sack of Rome?
I sit up late in Longley's little room
and listen to him conjugate, '*Amayo, amayas, amayat . . .*'

—

I look out the kitchen window. A cigarette burns
in the midst of the pyracanthus:
'What's with you, *a mhic?*
Apart from the 'eel-grass and bladderwrack'

there's not an image here that's worth a fuck.
Who gives a shit about the dreck

of your life? Who gives a toss
about your tossing off? 'I know, I know, but ... '

'But nothing : you know it's dross;
you know that 'Erasmus' stuff is an inept
attempt to cover your arse;

leave off your laundry-lists and tax-returns
and go back to making metaphors ... '
Something in that 'go back' reminds me of Xanthus.

The Mud Room

We followed the narrow track, my love, we followed the narrow
track through a valley in the Jura
to where the goats delight to tread upon the brink
of meaning. I carried my skating rink,
the folding one, plus
a pair of skates laced with convolvulus,
you a copy of the feminist Haggadah
from last year's Seder. I reached for the haggaday
or hasp over the half door of the mud room
in which, by and by, I grasped the rim
not of a quern or a chariot wheel but a wheel
of Morbier propped like the last reel
of *The Ten Commandments* or *The Robe*.
When she turned to us from high along the scarp
and showed us her gargoyle-
face stained with red-blue soil,
I could have sworn the she-goat was walking on air,
bounding, vaulting, pausing in mid-career
to browse on a sprig of the myrtle of which she's a devotee,
never putting a foot
wrong as she led us through the atrium's
down jackets, bow and quiver, jars of gefilte fish and garum,
to the uplands
where, at dusk, a farmer spreads a layer of bland
curds on the blue-green seam
of pine ash that runs like a schism
between bland dawn-milk and bland dusk-milk, along a corridor
smoking with the blue-green ordure
of cows, to yet another half door that would issue
on to the altar of Jehovah-nissi.
There are our kittens, Pangur Ban and Pyewacket,
sprawled on the horsehair blanket I bought in Bogotá

along with the horsehair hackamore.
There a wheel felloe of ash or sycamore
from the quadriga to which the steeds had no sooner been hitched
than it foundered in a blue-green ditch
with the rest of the Pharaoh's
war machine was perfectly preserved between two amphoras,
one of wild birdseed, the other of Kikkoman.
It was somewhere in this vicinity that I'd hidden the afikomen
at last year's Seder. I looked back down the Valley of the Kings
that was flooded now by the tears of things
and heard again that she-goat pipe
home a herd of cows, their hullabaloo and hubbub
at dawn or dusk, saw again her mouth stained with fraochans
(for she is of blaeberry browsers the paragon)
and followed her yet again through gefilte fish and garum jars,
crocks, cruses, saucepans, the samovar
from turn-of-the-century
Russia, along the blue-green path of pine cinders
through the myrtleberry—myrtle- or whortleberry?—underbrush
from which an apprehensive thrush
gave over its pre-emin . . . pre-emin . . . pre-emin . . .
its preeminent voice to *une petite chanson d'Allemagne.*
There, in the berry-laden scrub,
was a brangle of scrap
that had once been the body of that quadriga.
Yet again I stood amid the dreck
and clutter
of the mud room, the cardboard boxes from K-mart and Caldor,
the Hoover, the ironing board, the ram's horn
on which Moses called to Aaron, a pair of my da's boots so worn
it was hard to judge where the boots came to an end
and the world began, given how one would blend
imperceptibly into the other, given that there was no fine
blue-green line
between them. Virgil's *Georgics.* Plato's *Dialogues.*
Yet again the she-goat reared up on her hind legs
in the Jura or the Haute-Savoie

and perched on top of that amphora of soy
and stared across the ravine
that, imperceptibly, intervenes
between the stalwart curds of daybreak
onto which the farmer rakes
the pine coals from the warm hearthstone
and the stalwart curds of dailygone.
She reared up on her hind legs as if to see, once and for all,
the children of Israel negotiate the water wall
on their right hand
and on their left—"Look, no hands"—
as if a she-goat might indeed pause in mid-career to browse
on some horsehair blanket I bought in Valparaíso,
on a whirligig, a scythe and strickle, a cobbler's last.
They weighed on me now, the skating rink and the skates laced
with convolvulus as we followed the narrow track, my love,
to that rugged enclave
in the Jura, to where a she-goat might delight to tread
upon the middle cake of matzo bread
that runs as neat as neat
between unleavened morning and unleavened night.
Yet again that she-goat had run ahead
and yet again we followed her through the Haute-
Savoie past a ziggurat
of four eighty-pound bags of Sakrete,
on the top of which she paused to expose her red-blue tongue,
past the hearth set of brush, tongs
and poker bent
out of shape, past a shale outcrop of some of the preeminent
voices of the seventies—*The Pretender, Desperado, The Best of
    Spirit,*
box after cardboard box
of all manner of schmaltz and schlock from Abba to Ultravox,
till we heard the she-goat's own preeminent voice
from across the blue-green crevasse
that ran between the cohorts of dawn and the dusk cohorts,
heard her girn and grate

upon the mishegaas
of the brazen-mouthed cows
of morn and the brazen-mouthed cows of even,
their horns summoned up by a seven-
branched candlestick itself once or twice summoned up at Shabbat.
The candelabrum, the whirligig, those boots
with their toes worn through from the raking of pine coals
at crack of dawn and crepuscule,
the whirr of the bellows
and the dull glow
of pine ash, the hubcap from a Ford Sierra
blown up in—yes, sirree—
a controlled explosion in Belfast, the Kaliber six-pack,
the stack of twenty copies of *The Annals of Chile* ($21 hardback).
Again the she-goat would blare down the trail
when we paused to draw breath, as the children of Israel
might draw breath on the Sabbath,
again exhort us to follow the narrow path
that runs like a blue-green membrane
between the amphoras of soy and assorted small-headed grains,
exhort us yet again to follow
through the valley
"the narrow track to the highest good" as set forth by Epicurus,
past the hearth set of brush, tongs, and poker
bent out of shape, the ever-so-faint scent of musk,
till I happened upon the snow-swatch of damask
in which I'd wrapped the afikomen. The bag of pitons.
The medicinal bottle of poteen.
Yet again something had come between
the she-goat poised on a slope on which the cattle batten
and ourselves, that rivulet
or blue-green fault
between the clabber of morn and the stalwart even-clabber.
It was time, I felt sure, to unpack the Kaliber
into the old Hotpoint fridge
in which the she-goat was wont to forage,
to toss the poster tube—Hopper, Magritte, Grant Wood—

and clear a space in the dew-wet
underbrush in which, at long last, I might open
my folding skating rink and, at long last, tread upon
the hubcap of that old Sierra that could itself turn
on a sixpence, could itself turn
as precipitously as a bucket of milk in a booley-byre,
to roll up the strand of barbed wire
hand-wrought by the King of the Chaldeans,
the one and only Joseph Glidden,
that had run between the herd
of morn and the herd
of even, when you found the little *shuinshu* covered with black brocade
I bought for two Zuzim our last day in Kyoto
and it struck me that the she-goat
had somehow managed to acquire what looked like your skates
and your *gants en chevreau*
and was performing *grands jetés* on the hubcap of the Ford Zephyr.
I, meanwhile, was struggling for a foothold.
Even as I drove another pitton to the hilt
in the roughcast
of a bag of Sakrete, the she-goat executed an exquisite
suut de l'ange from an outcrop of shale,
pausing to browse on a sprig of myrtle or sweet gale
in the vicinity of the bow and quiver, down jackets, Hoover,
where I hid the afikomen last Passover,
bounding, vaulting, never making a slip
as I followed her, then as now—though then I had to schlep
through the brush of skirts (maxi- and mini-)
my folding rink plus my skates laced with scammony
plus the middle of the three
cakes of matzo bread that had, if you recall, since gone astray.
It was time, I felt sure, to unpack the Suntory
into the old fridge, to clear a space between *De Rerum Natura*
and Virgil's *Eclogues*,
a space in which, at long last, I might unlock
the rink, so I drove another piton into an eighty-pound
bag of Sakrete and flipped the half door on the dairy cabinet

126

of the old Hotpoint
and happened, my love, just happened
upon the cross
section of Morbier and saw, once and for all, the precarious
blue-green, pine-ash path along which Isaac followed Abraham
to an altar lit by a seven-branched candelabrum,
the ram's horn, the little goat whirligig
that left him all agog.

The Plot

He said, my pretty fair maid, if it is as you say,
I'll do my best endeavors in cutting of your hay,
For in your lovely countenance I never saw a frown,
So, my lovely lass, I'll cut your grass, that's ne'er been trampled down.

—TRADITIONAL BALLAD

```
a  l  f  a  l  f  a  l  f  a  l  f  a  l  f  a  l  f  a

l  f  a  l  f  a  l  f  a  l  f  a  l  f  a  l  f  a  l

f  a  l  f  a  l  f  a  l  f  a  l  f  a  l  f  a  l  f

a  l  f  a                             a  l  f  a

l  f  a  l                             l  f  a  l

f  a  l  f                             f  a  l  f

a  l  f  a           a  l  p  h  a      a  l  f  a

l  f  a  l                             l  f  a  l

f  a  l  f                             f  a  l  f

a  l  f  a                             a  l  f  a

l  f  a  l  f  a  l  f  a  l  f  a  l  f  a  l  f  a  l

f  a  l  f  a  l  f  a  l  f  a  l  f  a  l  f  a  l  f

a  l  f  a  l  f  a  l  f  a  l  f  a  l  f  a  l  f  a
```

Symposium

You can lead a horse to water but you can't make it hold
its nose to the grindstone and hunt with the hounds.
Every dog has a stitch in time. Two heads? You've been sold
one good turn. One good turn deserves a bird in the hand.

A bird in the hand is better than no bread.
To have your cake is to pay Paul.
Make hay while you can still hit the nail on the head.
For want of a nail the sky might fall.

People in glass houses can't see the wood
for the new broom. Rome wasn't built between two stools.
Empty vessels wait for no man.

A hair of the dog is a friend indeed.
There's no fool like the fool
who's shot his bolt. There's no smoke after the horse is gone.

from Sleeve Notes

CREAM: *Disraeli Gears*

As I laboured over the "Georgiks and Bukoliks"
I soon learned to tell thunder from dynamite.

THE ROLLING STONES: *Beggar's Banquet*

Thanks to Miss Latimore,
I was "coming along nicely" at piano

while, compared to the whoops and wild halloos
of the local urchins,

my diction
was im-pecc-a-ble.

In next to no time I would be lost
to the milk bars

and luncheonettes
of smoky Belfast,

where a troubadour
such as the frontman of Them

had long since traded in the lute
for bass and blues harmonica.

PINK FLOYD: *A Momentary Lapse of Reason*

We stopped in at a roadhouse on the way back from Lyonesse
and ordered a Tom Collins and an Old-Fashioned.
As we remounted the chariot

the poplar's synthesized alamo-alamo-eleison
was counterpointed by a redheaded woodpecker's rat-tat-tat
on a snare, a kettledrum's de dum de dum.

NIRVANA: *Bleach*

I went there, too, with Mona, or Monica.
Another shot of Absolut.

"The Wild Rover" or some folk anthem
on the jukebox. Some dour

bartender. I, too, have been held fast
by those snares and nets

off the Zinc Coast, the coast of Zanzibar,
                          lost

                able
                        addiction

            "chin-chins"
                        loos,

"And it's no,
nay, never, no nay never no more . . ."

A Journey to Cracow

As we hightailed it across the meadows
toward what might have been common ground
we were dragged down by our own shadows
through a dance floor near Wanda's mound

toward what might have been. Common ground?
Only when a black horse plunges
through a dance floor near Wanda's mound
do they take the barn door off its hinges,

only when a black horse plunges
into the Vistula swollen with rain
do they take the barn door off its hinges
to beat out the black grain.

Into the Vistula swollen with rain
you and I might have plunged and found a way
to beat out the black grain
as our forefathers did on threshing day,

you and I might have plunged and found a way
to set a cigarette on the barn door
as our forefathers did on threshing day
and dance rings around it forevermore,

to set a cigarette on the barn door
wherever it might be, for an instant even,
and dance rings around it forevermore
in some polka or Cracovienne,

whatever that might be. For an instant, even
we were dragged down by our own shadows,
my love, in some polka or mazurka or Cracovienne
as we hightailed it across the meadows.

A Half Door near Cluny

s t a b l e s t a b l e s t a b l e s

t a b l e s t a b l e s t a b l e s t

a b l e s t a b l e s t a b l e s t a

b l e s   s t a b

l e s t   t a b l

e s t a   a b l e

s t a b   b l e s

t a b l   b l é   l e s t

a b l e   e s t a

b l e s   s t a b

l e s t   t a b l

e s t a   a b l e

s t a b l e s t a b l e s t a b l e s

t a b l e s t a b l e s t a b l e s t

a b l e s t a b l e s t a b l e s t a

b l e s t a b l e s t a b l e s t a b

l e s t a b l e s t a b l e s t a b l

e s t a b l e s t a b l e s t a b l e

s t a b l e s t a b l e s t a b l e s

Hard Drive

With my back to the wall
and a foot in the door
and my shoulder to the wheel
I would drive through Seskinore.

With an ear to the ground
and my neck on the block
I would tend to my wound
in Belleek and Bellanaleck.

With a toe in the water
and a nose for trouble
and an eye to the future
I would drive through Derryfubble

and Dunnamanagh and Ballynascreen,
keeping that wound green.

Winter Wheat

I

The plowboy was something his something as I nibbled
    the lobe
of her right ear and something her blouse
for the Empire-blotchy globe
of her left breast on which there something a something
    louse.

II

Those something lice like something seed-pearls
and her collar something with dandruff
as when Queen Elizabeth entertained the Earls
in her something something ruff.

III

I might have something the something groan
of the something plowboy who would with such
    something urge
the something horses, a something and a roan,
had it not been for the something splurge
of something like the hare
which even now managed to something itself from the
    something plowshare.

As

As naught gives way to aught
and ox-hide gives way to chain-mail
and byrnie gives way to battle-ax
and Cavalier gives way to Roundhead
and Cromwell Road gives way to the Connaught
and *I am Curious (Yellow)* gives way to *I am Curious (Blue)*
and barrelhouse gives way to Frank'n'Stein
and a pint of Shelley plain to a pint of India Pale Ale
I give way to you.

As bass gives way to baritone
and hammock gives way to hummock
and Hoboken gives way to Hackensack
and bread gives way to reed bed
and bald eagle gives way to Theobald Wolfe Tone
and the Undertones give way to Siouxsie Sioux
and DeLorean, John, gives way to Deloria, Vine,
and Pierced Nose to Big Stomach
I give way to you.

As vent gives way to Ventury
and the King of the World gives way to Finn MacCool
and phone gives way to fax
and send gives way to sned
and Dagenham gives way to Coventry
and Covenanter gives way to caribou
and the caribou gives way to the carbine
and Boulud's cackamamie to the cock-a-leekie of Boole
I give way to you.

As transhumance gives way to trance
and shaman gives way to Santa
and butcher's string gives way to vacuum pack
and the ineffable gives way to the unsaid
and pyx gives way to monstrance
and treasure aisle gives way to need-blind pew
and Calvin gives way to Calvin Klein
and Town and Country Mice to Hanta
I give way to you.

As Hopi gives way to Navaho
and rug gives way to rag
and *Pax Vobiscum* gives way to Tampax
and Tampa gives way to the water bed
and *The Water Babies* gives way to *Worstward Ho*
and crapper gives way to loo
and spruce gives way to pine
and the carpet of pine-needles to the carpetbag
I give way to you.

As gombeen-man gives way to not-for-profit
and soft soap gives way to Lynn C. Doyle
and tick gives way to tack
and Balaam's Ass gives way to Mister Ed
and *Songs of Innocence* gives way to *The Prophet*
and single-prop Bar-B-Q gives way to twin-screw
and The Salt Lick gives way to The County Line
and 'Mending Wall' gives way to 'Build Soil'
I give way to you.

As your hummus gives way to your foul madams
and your coy mistress gives way to 'The Flea'
and flax gives way to W. D. Flackes
and the living give way to the dead
and John Hume gives way to Gerry Adams

and Television gives way to U2
and Lake Constance gives way to the Rhine
and the Rhine to the Zuider Zee
I give way to you.

As dutch treat gives way to french leave
and spanish fly gives way to Viagra
and slick gives way to slack
and the local fuzz give way to the Feds
and Machiavelli gives way to make believe
and *Howards End* gives way to *A Room with a View*
and Wordsworth gives way to 'Woodbine
Willie' and stereo Nagra to quad Niagara
I give way to you.

As cathedral gives way to cavern
and cookie cutter gives way to cookie
and the rookies give way to the All Blacks
and the shad give way to the smoke shed
and the rough-shod give way to the Black Horse   avern
that still rings true
despite that 'T' being missing from its sign
where a little nook gives way to a little nookie
when I give way to you.

That *Nanook of the North* should give way to *Man of Aran*
as ling gives way to cod
and cod gives way to kayak
and Camp Moosilauke gives way to Club Med
and catamite gives way to catamaran
and catamaran to aluminum canoe
is symptomatic of a more general decline
whereby a cloud succumbs to a clod
and I give way to you.

For as Monet gives way to Juan Gris
and Juan Gris gives way to Joan Miró
and Metro-Goldwyn-Mayer gives way to Miramax
and the Volta gives way to Travolta, swinging the red-hot lead,
and *Saturday Night Fever* gives way to *Grease*
and the Greeks give way to you know who
and the Roman IX gives way to the Arabic 9
and nine gives way, as ever, to zero
I give way to you.

from Horse Latitudes

BEIJING

I could still hear the musicians
cajoling those thousands of clay
horses and horseman through the squeeze
when I woke beside Carlotta.
Life-size, also. Also terra-cotta.
The sky was still a terra-cotta frieze
over which her grandfather still held sway
with the set square, fretsaw, stencil,
plumb line, and carpenter's pencil
his gradfather brought from Roma.
Proud-fleshed Carlotta. Hypersarcoma.
For now our highest ambition
was simply to bear the light of the day
we had once been planning to seize.

BAGINBUN

The Nashville skyline's hem and haw
as the freebooters who freeboot
through their contractual mire and murk,
like Normans stampeding dozens
of cows into their Norse-Irish cousins,
were balking now at this massive breastwork
they themselves had thrown up. The pile of toot
on a mirror. The hip-hirple
of a white horse against purple.
Age-old traductions I could trace
from freebasers pretending they freebase
to this inescapable flaw
hidden by Carlotta's close-knit wet suit
like a heart-wound by a hauberk.

BANNOCKBURN

Though he was mounted on a cob
rather than a warhorse, the Bruce
still managed to sidestep a spear
from Henry de Bohun and tax
de Bohun's poll with his broad-based poleax
and leave de Bohun's charger somewhat leer.
Her grandfather had yet to find a use
for the two-timing partisan
his grandfather brought man-to-man
against all those Ferdinandies
until he saw it might come in handy
for whacking the thingammybobs
off pine and fir, off pine and fir and spruce
and all such trees as volunteer.

BLACKWATER FORT

As I had held Carlotta close
that night we watched some Xenophon
embedded with the 5th Marines
in the old Sunni Triangle
make a half-assed attempt to untangle
the ghastly from the price of gasoline.
There was a distant fanfaron
in the Nashville sky, where the wind
had now drawn itself up and pinned
on her breast a Texaco star.
"Why," Carlotta wondered, "the House of *Tar*?
Might it have to do with the gross
imports of crude oil Bush will come clean on
only when the Tigris comes clean?"

BLENHEIM

Small birds were sounding the alert
as I followed her unladen
steed through a dell so dark and dank
she might have sported the waders
her grandfather had worn at the nadir
of his career, scouring the Outer Banks
for mummichog and menhaden.
Those weeks and months in the doldrums
coming back as he ran his thumb
along an old venetian blind
in the hope that something might come to mind,
that he might yet animadvert
the maiden name of that Iron Maiden
on which he was drawing a blank.

BUNKER HILL

Carlotta took me in her arms
as a campfire gathers a branch
to itself, her mouth a cauter
set to my bleeding bough, heehaw.
Her grandfather sterilizing his saw
in a tub of 100-proof firewater,
a helper standing by to stanch
the bleeding in some afterlife.
No looking daggers at the knife.
She'd meet the breast-high parapet
with the nonchalance, the no fucking sweat
of a slightly skanky schoolmarm
though the surgeon was preparing to ganch
her like What's-his-face's Daughter.

BRONKHORSTSPRUIT

I traced the age-old traduction
of a stream through a thorn thicket
as a gush from a farthingale.
Skeffington's Daughter. *Skeffington.*
Attention. Shun. Attention. Shun. Shun. Shun.
We lay in a siding between two rails
and watched an old white horse cross the picket
of himself and trek though the scrub
to drink from an iron-hooped tub
with the snore-snort of a tuba.
His winkers and bellyband said scuba,
while his sudden loss of suction
Carlotta knew meant a pump whose clicket's
failed in the way a clicket fails.

BAZENTIN

As I was bringing up her rear
a young dragoon would cock a snook
at the gunners raking the knob
of High Wood. Tongue like a scaldy
in a nest. Hadn't a Garibaldi
what might lie behind that low-level throb
like a niggle in her appointment book.
Dust? Fust? Must? The dragoon nonplussed
by his charger taking the rust
and, despite her racalcitrance,
Carlotta making a modest advance
when the thought of a falchioneer
falling to with his two-faced reaping hook
now brought back her grandfather's job.

144

Tithonus

Not the day-old cheep of a smoke detector on the blink
in what used to be the root cellar,
or the hush-hush of all those drowsy syrups
against their stoppers

in the apothecary chest
at the far end of your grandmother's attic,
nor the "my sweet, my sweet"
of ice branch frigging ice branch,

nor the jinkle-jink
of your great-grandfather, the bank teller
who kept six shots of medicinal (he called it "therap-
utraquist") whiskey like six stacks of coppers

stacked against him by the best
and the brightest of the American Numismatic
Society from the other side of 155th Street,
nor the in-the-silence-after-the-horse-avalanche

spur-spink
heard by your great-great-grandfather, the Rebel yeller
who happened to lose a stirrup
and come a cropper

at the very start of the Confederate offensive in the west,
nor even the phatic
whittering of your great-great-grandmother ("such a good *seat*")
whose name was, of all things, Blanche,

nor again the day-old cheep of a smoke detector on the blink
in what used to be the root cellar
but what turns out to be the two-thousand-year-old chirrup
of a grasshopper.

Bob Dylan at Princeton, November 2000

We cluster at one end, one end of Dillon Gym.
"You know what, honey? We call that a homonym."

We cluster at one end, one end of the Dillon Gym.
"If it's fruit you're after, you go out on a limb."

That last time in Princeton, that ornery degree,
those seventeen-year locusts hanging off the trees.

The last time in Princeton, that ornery degree,
his absolute refusal to bend the knee.

His last time in Princeton, he wouldn't wear a hood.
Now he's dressed up as some sort of cowboy dude.

That last time in Princeton, he wouldn't wear a hood.
"You know what, honey? We call that disquietude.

It's that self-same impulse that has him rearrange
both 'The Times They Are A-Changin' ' and 'Things Have Changed'

so that everything seems to fall within his range
as the locusts lock in on grain silo and grange."

The Outlier

I

In Armagh or Tyrone
I fell between two stones.

In Armagh or Tyrone
on a morning in June
I fell between two stones.

In Armagh or Tyrone
on a morning in June
in 1951
I fell between two stones.

In Armagh or Tyrone
on a morning in June
in 1951
I fell between two stones
that raised me as their own.

II

I had one eye, just one,
they prised and propped open.

I had one eye, just one,
they prised and propped open
like a Fomorian's.

I had one eye, just one,
they prised and propped open

like a Fomorian's
with a fire-toughened pine.

I had one eye, just one,
they prised and propped open
like a Fomorian's
so all I looked upon
would itself turn to stone.

Flags and Emblems

What to make of your quickie
with some moonlighting Provo or Stickie
who did you over, whoah, did you over,
till your blue-black hickey

Riddle-me-O
Riddle-me-O

ran like mascara?
Or the former members of Tara
who lured you into their new Land Rover
with a couple of ex-Paras

Riddle-me-O
Riddle-me-O

turned paper hangers
and dumped you in a cornfield sangar
(that little hip trench lined with stover
to soften the blow to gangbangers)

Riddle-me-O
Riddle-me-O

like a deer dumped in her own numbles?
Not even the fee-fie-fo-fumble
of a giant cattle drover
with whom you had a little rough and tumble

Riddle-me-O
Riddle-me-O

amid a roundabout's right-as-rain azaleas
can account for the regalia
with its leitmotif of a four-leaf clover
you've worn each year at the great Terminalia

O-riddle-me-O
Riddle-me-riddle-me-O.

Riddle

My first may be found, if found it ever is, quite firmly embedded in grime
but not in rime,
despite the fact that I'm
cold as well as dirty, what with being stowed away almost all the time.

My second sounds doubly in roar
and singly in oar.
When the buccaneers put ashore
and set fire to our little craft, my spirit would sink, then soar

when I thought of my third, found in the ideal
but not in the raw deal
I got from them. Just because I've a heart of steel
doesn't mean I don't *feel*.

My fourth is in Drake
but not in rake.
They'd rake the coals they'd make me walk. My last request was for a steak
followed by something like a piece of cake.

My fifth is in drum
but not in rum.
The drunken buccaneers offered me a lump of dough if I'd keep mum.
A lump in my throat. My lump sum.

My sixth is in leaves
but not in eaves.
I overheard them laughing about "honour among thieves"
when they left me stranded here with the dry heaves.

My last heaves to, as it were, twice in event
but once only in vent.

I'm still wearing that old stovepipe hat. I've made scarcely a dent
in that lump of dough I was given, or lent,

by the buccaneers from whom I still take my cue.
A barb of smoke from the barbecue
brings a blush to the cheek of the cockatoo
who'll wait as long for a word from me as I'll wait for a word from you.

The Mountain is Holding Out

The mountain is holding out
for news from the sea
of the raid on the redoubt.
The plain won't level with me

for news from the sea
is harder and harder to find.
The plain won't level with me
now it's nonaligned

and harder and harder to find.
The forest won't fill me in
now it, too, is nonaligned
and its patience wearing thin.

The forest won't fill me in
or the lake confess
to its patience wearing thin.
I'd no more try to guess

why the lake might confess
to a regard for its own sheen,
no more try to guess
why the river won't come clean

on its regard for its own sheen
than why you and I've faced off across a ditch.
For the river not coming clean
is only one of the issues on which

you and I've faced off across a ditch
and the raid on the redoubt
only one of the issues on which
the mountain is holding out.

Hedge School

Not only those rainy mornings our great-great-grandmother was
    posted at a gate
with a rush mat
over her shoulders, a mat that flashed
Papish like a heliograph, but those rainy mornings when my
    daughter and the rest

of her all-American Latin class may yet be forced to conjugate
Guantánamo, amas, amat
and learn with Luciana how "headstrong liberty is lash'd
with woe"—all past and future mornings were impressed

on me just now, dear Sis,
as I sheltered in a doorway on Church Street in St. Andrews
(where, in 673, another Maelduin was bishop),

and tried to come up with a ruse
for unsealing the *New Shorter English Dictionary* back in that corner
    shop
and tracing the root of *metastasis*.

Three Plows

There are three plows on the New Jersey seal
And they're plowing me right under
Three plows breaking the frozen soil
In the dead of winter
The first plow came with a halter
I strung around my neck
I climbed the corporate ladder
A corporate exec
Till they caught me trying to steal
From a corporate funder
And those three plows on the New Jersey seal
Were plowing me right under

There are three plows on the New Jersey seal
And they're plowing me right under
It being ripped right off the soul
Leaves a body tender
I'm still bloody from the sentence
Handed down by Judge Cook
In the courthouse back in Trenton
Where I was brought to book
No more Chambersburg no more breaded veal
No more Trenton Thunder
There are three plows on the New Jersey seal
And they're plowing me right under

There are three plows on the New Jersey seal
And they're plowing me right under
It might look like I'm lounging in my cell
With *American Venture*
But I've been pondering those plowshares
For five years in Fort Dix

Was it back there on the bleachers
Chicken wings and cheese sticks
Or as I stood in the Court of Appeals
I first began to wonder
If those three plows on the New Jersey seal
Weren't plowing me right under?

Macgillycuddy's Reeks

She stood beside my narrow bed
To check my EKG
She shook her pretty little head
At what's become of me
I thought I glimpsed a path that led
Through rhododendron days
And fuchsia nights to the boat shed
In which we two once lay

But she gazed only at my chart
The valleys and the peaks
Brought back the time she broke my heart
In Macgillycuddy's Reeks
But she gazed only at my chart
The valleys and the peaks
Brought back the time she broke my heart
In Macgillycuddy's Reeks

I saw her on Killarney's shore
One morning in July
When I still thought I was a thorn
Trying to find a side
I met her in the little launch
That runs to Innisfallen
Hunched together haunch to haunch
Trying to keep my balance

But she upset my applecart
She kissed me on the cheek
And I was struck by Cupid's dart
In Macgillycuddy's Reeks
Macgillycuddy's Reeks

Macgillycuddy's Reeks
I was struck by Cupid's dart
In Macgillycuddy's Reeks

She was a systems analyst
For a dot com company
She said you think because we've kissed
I'll be yours eternally
I'll sign another pre-nup
And we'll merge our PLCs
That's why most girls go belly up
In this economy

And when it comes to a jump-start
Your forecast's pretty bleak
The Nasdaq goes by fits and starts
Like Macgillycuddy's Reeks
Macgillycuddy's Reeks
Macgillycuddy's Reeks
The Nasdaq goes by fits and starts
Like Macgillycuddy's Reeks

She gazed only at my chart
The valleys and the peaks
Brought back the time she broke my heart
In Macgillycuddy's Reeks
Macgillycuddy's Reeks
Macgillycuddy's Reeks
That was the time she broke my heart
In Macgillycuddy's Reeks

Come Close

To think you used to mock
Me for saying Woodstock
And three-car-garage rock
Are both somewhat grandiose
That Victoria Gotti
And J Paul Getty
And Buanarroti
And Giacometti
Are chips off the old block

You said they don't come close
They don't even come close

To think you used to scold
Me for saying *Das Rhinegold*
And *Tristan und Isolde*
Are both somewhat grandiose
My saying Paris Hilton
And Haile Selassie
And Carrière's *Milton*
And your own sweet chassis
Were cast in the same mold

You said they don't come close
They don't even come close

To the night you said
Wall Street was in bed
With the SEC
That's right the night you said
Wall Street was in bed
With the SEC

You said don't come close
Don't even come close to me

To think you used to scoff
At my saying Philip Roth
And the Pink Floyd behemoth
Were both somewhat grandiose
My saying the Dalai Lama
And Andrew Carnegie
And the orange pajamas
That make you look so leggy
Are cut from the same cloth

You said they don't come close
They don't even come close

Going through the Hoops

When I sang flat out in that prog rock group
It was all soft drugs it was all soft porn
All duping the dupes all duping the dupes
I lay with Ruth in the alien corn
Dusting down the crop circles by the hawthorns
Going through going through going through the hoops

When I flew flat out in that airshow troupe
She was all windswept I was all windshorn
All looping the loop all looping the loop
I married Ruth one Abingdon Fayre morn
Arching under the sabres with our newborn
Going through going through going through the hoops

Ruth and I were downsized and outsourced
No more where's the kief no more bhang for your buck
No more horsing around with the Royal Air Force
When we ran into Duxford we ran right out of luck
No more going berserk no more running amuck
Struck off like Yorkshire fog from the Gog Magog Golf Course

One kid with whooping cough the other with croup
Going through going through going through the hoops

Now I lie flat out for the *Sunday Snoop*
It's all hard drugs it's all hard porn
All scooping the poop all scooping the poop
Ruth and I who dreamed of the Gates of Horn
Playing to-the-death croquet weekends in Bourne
Our hopes forlorn our dreams outworn
Going through going through going through the hoops

My Ride's Here

(with Warren Zevon)

I was staying at the Marriott
With Jesus and John Wayne
I was waiting for a chariot
They were waiting for a train
The sky was full of carrion
I'll take the mazuma
Said Jesus to Marion
That's the 3:10 to Yuma
My ride's here

The Houston sky was changeless
We galloped through bluebonnets
I was wrestling with an angel
You were working on a sonnet
You said I believe the seraphim
Will gather up my pinto
And carry us away Jim
Across the San Jacinto
My ride's here

Shelley and Keats were out on the street
And even Lord Byron was leaving for Greece
While back at the Hilton last but not least
Milton was holding his sides
Saying you bravos had better be ready to fight
Or we'll never get out of East Texas tonight
For the trail is long and the river is wide
And my ride's here

I was staying at the Westin
I was playing to a draw
When in walked Charlton Heston

164

With the Tablets of the Law
He said it's still the Greatest Story
I said man I'd like to stay
But I'm bound for glory
I'm on my way
My ride's here

Plan B

I

On my own head be it if, after the years of elocution and pianoforte,
the idea that I may have veered

away from the straight
and narrow of Brooklyn or Baltimore for a Baltic state

is one at which, all things being equal, I would demur.
A bit like Edward VII cocking his ear

at the mention of Cork. Yet it seems I've managed nothing more
than to have fetched up here.

II

To have fetched up here in Vilna – the linen plaids,
the amber, the orange-cap boletus

like a confession extorted from a birch,
the foot-wide pedestal upon which a prisoner would perch

on one leg in the former KGB headquarters
like a white stork

before tipping into a pool of icy water,
to be reinstated more than once by a guard with a pitchfork.

III

It was with a pitchfork they prodded Topsy, the elephant
that killed her keeper on Coney Island

when he tried to feed her a lit cigarette,
prodded her through Luna Park in her rain-heavy skirt

to where she would surely have been hanged by the neck
had the ASPCA not got themselves into such a lather

and Thomas Edison arrived in the nick
of time to greet the crowd he'd so long hoped to gather.

IV

I myself have been trying to gather the dope
from a KGB surveillance tape

on the Chazon Ish, 'the wisest Jew alive', a master of the catchall
clause who was known to cudgel

his brains in a room high in a Vilna courtyard
on the etymology of 'dork'

while proposing that the KGB garotte
might well be a refinement of the Scythian torc.

V

The Scythian torc had already been lent a new lease
of life as the copper wire with which Edison would splice

Topsy to more than 6000 volts of alternating current,
though not before he'd prepared the ground

with a boatload of carrots laced with cyanide.
This was 1903. The year in which Edward VII paid

out a copper line from his mustachioed snout
to the electric chair where Edison himself was now belayed.

VI

Now a belayed, bloody prisoner they've put on the spot
and again and again zapped

is the circus rider on a dappled
croup from which he's more than once toppled

into the icy water, spilling his guts
about how his grandfather had somehow fetched up in Cork

straight from the Vilno ghetto,
having misheard, it seems, 'Cork' for 'New York'.

VII

For New York was indeed the city in which the floor teetered
at a ball thrown in 1860 in honor of Edward

(then Prince of Wales), the city in which even I may have put
myself above all those trampled underfoot,

given my perfect deportment all those years I'd skim
over the dying and the dead

looking up to me as if I might at any moment succumb
to the book balanced on my head.

Maggot

I

I used to wait on a motorcade
to stretch to the world rim.
Now I've been left in the shade
with only this slim jim.

I used to wait for a moonless night
before parachuting in.
Now it's come to light
I've spread myself too thin

where I'm waiting for some lover
to kick me out of bed
for having acted on a whim

when the yarrow opened its two-page spread
and the trout stirred from its hover
under a brook brim.

II

I used to wait for the dawn raid
where gloom gave way to glim
and packed the parachute I'd paid
out like the flim-

flammable box kite
of a wild boar's intestine.
Often an acolyte
will be taking it on the chin

where I'm waiting for some lover
to kick me out of bed
for having acted on a whim

in the scriptorium I fled
when a limestone coffer
was let slip by two seraphim.

III

I used to wait, undaunted, undismayed,
where one trout held on like grim
death to a frayed
leader while another would skim

the Personals in the hope she might ignite
the fire within.
Now I've taken the fight
to an identical twin

where I'm waiting for some lover
to kick me out of bed
for having acted on a whim

with the aforesaid
trout who was all in a pother
while pretending to be prissy-prim.

IV

I used to be somehwat swayed
by an Italian patronym.
Now the Val Cordevole brigade
holds firm at the gym.

I used to have an appetite
for wild boar in gin.
Now I take a sound bite
with a mic on a tiepin

where I'm waiting for some lover
to kick me out of bed
for having acted on a whim

with that Miss Trifoglio who led
me to believe I'd be 'in clover'
now her main ingredient was Pimm's.

V

I used to wait in the colonnade
while a poplar got a trim
or watched as a partisan was flayed
with such vigor and vim

it no longer seemed a fancy-flight
to fancy my arm a fin.
Now I'm buoyant despite
having taken another tailspin

where I'm waiting for some lover
to kick me out of bed
for having acted on a whim,

her tongue livid with pencil lead
like the partisan I knew as a pencil shover
who dangles still by one limb.

VI

I used to admire a peasant maid
through her dimity-dim.
Now I ply my trade
in the interim

between dropping into the Dolomites
on a clandestine
mission and the breach site
I've yet to win

where I'm waiting for some lover
to kick me out of bed
for having acted on a whim

as unpremeditatedly as the pretty pre-med
who proved to be such a pushover
now she'd passed her prelims.

VII

I used to wait for the serenade
of a fly choir singing a fly hymn
without the visual aid
of the rubric some monk might limn

from carmine and graphite
bound in albumin.
Now I'm content to write
to her next of kin

where I'm waiting for some lover
to kick me out of bed
for having acted on a whim,

having been given up for dead
like so many left to smother
behind the chemise scrim.

VIII

I used to wait while a trout inveighed
against the yarrow corymb
as the birch will upbraid
the fly agaric with which it has a sym-

biotic relationship. Has-been is tight
with has-been.
An ex-Franciscan will plight
his troth to an ex-Ursuline

where I'm waiting for some lover
to kick me out of bed
for having acted on a whim

and quibbled with Miss Trifoglio instead
of taking up the offer
of her little Commie quim.

IX

I used to wait for another ambuscade
with only my hotwire shim.
Now I'm no less a blade
than Pistol, Bardolph or Nym.

I used to think the partisans wore white
because they were free of sin.
Now I think it only right
to have got beneath her skin

where I'm waiting for some lover
to kick me out of bed
for having acted on a whim

when she herself has taken it into her head
all those who've gone undercover
may as well sink as swim.

The Rowboat

I

Every year he'd sunk
the old, clinker-built rowboat
so it might again float.
Every year he'd got drunk

as if he might once and for all write off
every year he'd sunk,
kerplunk, kerplunk,
one after another into a trough

no water would staunch.
Like a waterlogged tree trunk,
every year he'd sunk
just as he was about to launch

into a diatribe on the chunk
of change this bitch
was costing him, the debt into which
every year he'd sunk.

II

The old, clinker-built rowboat
with its shriveled strakes
would be immersed in the lake,
the lake that itself rewrote

many a stage play for the big screen.
The old, clinker-built rowboat

in which he'd stashed the ice tote
from L. L. Bean

for Crested Ten on the rocks
(one part Crested Ten, two parts creosote),
the old, clinker-built rowboat
he'd threatened to leave on the dock

and give a coat
of varnish that would somehow clinch the deal,
that would once and for all seal
the old, clinker-built rowboat.

III

So it might again float
the possibility one must expand
with Coutts and Co. (without the ampersand),
misquoting them as one might misquote

the price of Paramount stock
so it might again float.
More than once he'd written a promissory note
and put himself in hock

more than once to assuage
the fears for a property expressed by the Coutthroats
so it might again float
from the big screen to the stage

and gain by losing something of its bloat,
taking as he did the chance
it might be imbued with some new significance
so it might again float.

176

IV

Every year he'd got drunk
and railed at this one and that,
the baseball birdbrain, the basketball gnat,
the gin-soaked punk

he threatened with a punching out of lights
every year he'd got drunk,
the Coutts & Co. quidnunc
whose argument was no more watertight

than any by which he might inure
himself against the basketball gnat's slam dunk.
Every year he'd got drunk
but resisted taking a cure

just as every year he'd shrunk
from the thought, kerpow,
he'd most likely go under given how
every year he'd got drunk.

Lines for the Centenary
of the Birth of Samuel Beckett

I

Only now do we see how each crossroads
was bound to throw up not just a cross
but a couple of gadabouts with goads,
a couple of gadabouts at a loss

as to why they were at the beck and call
of some old crock soaring above the culch
of a kitchen midden at evenfall,
some old crock roaring across the gulch

as a hanged man roars out to a hanged man.
Now bucket nods to bucket of the span
of an ash yoke, or something of that ilk . . .

Now one hanged man kicks at the end of his rope
in another little attack of hope.
Now a frog in one bucket thickens the milk.

II

Now a frog in one bucket thickens the milk
as it tries out for the sublime
from chime to birch-wood chime,
a frog thrown in with no more thought as to whilk

way he was geen
from the hussy turned resourceful housewife
than she gave to where in Ayreshire or Fife
her beloved spalpeen

might fetch up as a tatie-hoker,
a tatie-hoker revealing a lining of red tatted silk
of his sackcloth, so to speak,

just as it's revealed our stockbroker
is creaming off five hundred a week
while the frog in one bucket thickens the milk.

III

Now a frog in one bucket thickens the milk
as a heart might quicken behind its stave
at the thought of a thief who bilked
us of our life savings himself being saved.

Only now do we see ... How spasm and lull
are mirrored somewhat by lull and spasm
when the nitwit roars out to the numbskull
thinking he might yet narrow the chasm

between his own cask and the other's keg,
thinking he might take the other down a peg
if not leave him completely in the lurch ...

Leave him to ponder if it's less an ash
yoke tipped by his bucket of balderdash,
less an ash yoke than a crossbar of birch.

IV

Less an ash yoke than a crossbar of birch
from the single birch that insinuated itself into the grove
of oaks sacred to Jove
and took him in as from his perch

the nincompoop who's churning our account
took in the other knucklehead
with the proposal that our aversion to being bled
is pretty much tantamount

to the old crock being averse to paying his ransom,
the bucket where you would search
for the significance of a frog taking the plunge

proving to be less cask than keg, the transom
from which the old crock offered his vinegar sponge
less an ash yoke than a crossbar of birch.

V

Less an ash yoke than a crossbar of birch
and a birch-wood bucket where a frog breasts
the very milk we feared it would besmirch.
Only now do we see we're at the behest

not of some old crock kicking the beam
but ourselves. We balk at the idea, balk
at the idea of a frog no sooner opening a seam
in milk than it's ... Surely not *caulked*?

Only now do we see how it's ourselves who skim
determinedly through the dim
of evenfall with no more regard for our load

as we glance up through the sky hoop
than the ninny who roars back to the nincompoop,
'Only now do we see how each crossroads ...'

At the Lab

Somewhere off the Grand Banks
a lapstrake sea that sailed into the teeth
of a gale now foundered on a reef
and promptly sank.

I was at the lab to analyze the spore
in a seaweed wreath
marking the spot where it came to grief,
you the pollen in a sediment core

from a bog in Ireland where, thanks
to its being built plank-upon-plank
(each rig fastened to the one beneath),

a plowed field running alongside the shore
had reached North America before
Eric or Leif.

Federico García Lorca: "Death"

What a tremendous effort they all put into it!
The horse does its damnedest
to become a dog.
The dog tries so hard to become a swallow.
The swallow busies itself with becoming a bee.
The bee does its level best to become a horse.
As for the horse,
just look at the barbed arrow it draws from the rose,
that faint rose lifting from its underlip.
The rose meanwhile,
what a slew of lights and calls
are bound up in the living sugar of its stem.
The sugar in turn,
those daggers it conjures while standing watch.
The little daggers themselves,
such a moon minus horse stalls, such nakedness,
such robust and ruddy skin as they're bent upon.
And I, perched on the gable-end,
what a blazing angel I aim at being, and am.
The arch made of plaster, however –
how huge, how invisible, then how small it is,
without the least striving.

Seven Selfies from the Château d'If

1

I too was flung into a cell so dark
I'd hunger for the black and moldy bread
that all too soon defined my comfort zone.
I cast my mind back for some ill-judged phrase,
unguarded look, circumstance I'd misread,
some vibe I gave at which some took offence.

2

I too have heard another scratch his mark
with such conviction as might match my own.

3

I too was schooled by a high-minded monk
who ruled the world-book must be read aloud.

4

It took both winter freeze and summer freeze
to yield growth-rings so uniformly dense
my tone brought back a Stradivarius –
demure-insistent, delicate-immense.

5

I too switched with a dead man in his bunk
and stitched myself into his burlap shroud.

6

I too have heard ghoulish pallbearers scoff
while I've kept cool and clutched my toothbrush shank.

7

I too am hurtling down with such great force
it's even harder to keep playing dead
while knowing in my bones I shouldn't tense
myself for impact. Soon I will slit the cloth
and, having freed one arm, then free my head
and hope to surface far from where I sank.

The Firing Squad

*I am going to tell you something I never but once let out of the bag before
and that was just after I reached London and before I had begun to value
myself for what I was worth. It is a very damaging secret and you may not
thank me for taking you into it when I tell you I have often wished I could
be sure that the other sharer of it had perished in the war. It is this: The
poet in me died nearly ten years ago.*

Robert Frost to Louis Untermeyer, May 4 1916

I am very happy I am dying for the glory of God and the honour of Ireland.

Joseph Mary Plunkett to Father Sebastian, May 4 1916

Something I never but once let on
is that I am as ready to be hanged, drawn,
and quartered as the Blessed Oliver, as ready as his sober-suited
descendant, Joseph Mary Plunkett,
to be shot – all the more so if I've married my beloved Grace
only hours before. Like many of my race,
I've come to see English plantain as a flatfooted
weed terminating in an oblongoid

spike of flowers like the head of a mace.
It tends to establish itself in the least likely place,
exercising a feudal
droit de seigneur on pavements, parking lots where battery
acid and diesel have bled
into the soil, drive-ins where we're wooed by, and wed
to, the whole kit and caboodle
of empire. As for a priest or padre

laying about him with his holy-water sprinkler, it has me see red

no less than if he wielded a flint ax-head

made by an old-style flint knapper.

That's why I get up from my pillow (filled, as it happens, with buckwheat),

to set my face against the dawn.

As I stride out now across the Institute lawn

I look all the more dapper

for the white handkerchief so firmly lodged in my breast pocket.

Álvaro De Campos: "Belfast, 1922"

While a great gantry
at the head of the Lough
continues to stand sentry
a team of shipyard men rush to caulk

a seam. No dunnock in a choir
of dunnocks will relent
from claiming as its own the gore
of land on which Harland

& Wolff is built. Catching a rivet
in a pair of tongs
and banging it into a rift
will hardly mend it. The dun in *dun*nock

doesn't allow for the dash
of silver in its head and throat feathers.
Because chicks within one clutch
often have different fathers,

dunnocks are at once highly territorial
and likely to go unremarked.
Though they've been known to drill
in Glenavy and Deer Park,

the dunchered shipyard men are no less peaceable
than those of Barrow-in-Furness.
Souped-up, staid, swerveless, supple,
they hold in equal reverence

the pennywhistle and the plenilunar
pigskin of a Lambeg drum,
be they sending off a White Star liner
or a little tramp.

Los Dissidentes

Coming to anything late in the day has an allure
all its own. The river plummets here with such aplomb
it brings back Slim Pickens's holler
as he bronco-busts the H-Bomb

in *Dr. Strangelove.* We like it when things are stacked
against us, when beavers are showing
initiative at the beaver dam. We take comfort from the fact
that after years of scenery-chewing

Rockets Redglare thoroughly upped
his profile with his role in *Down By Law.*
Though the file

is almost certainly corrupt,
we can still hope to salvage something from the raw
footage of the waterfall.

Noah & Sons

1

A solitary ewe stood guard
like a widow in her mantle
at the entrance to the graveyard.
One line ran all the way from my pommel through my cantle

to the Massey Ferguson baler
while lovers screamed with tumult harsh
and a converted whaler
sank slowly into the alder marsh.

As we cantered across the stubble
we managed to double
back on ourselves like hares
fleeing a primal scene
to which we're bound to repair
as long as yellow + blue = green.

2

For "ewe" read "yew."
For "baler" read "thrasher."
For "retina" read "retinue."
For "Ashur" read "Asher."

For "fathead" read "minnow."
For "shame" read "Shem."
For "window" read "winnow."
For "bract" read "stem."

For "missile" read "Missal."
For "darnel" read "thistle."
For "skewered" read "skewed."
For "hart" read "chart."
For "Freud" read "feud."
For "dirt" read "dart."

3

Now we were galloping across the swamp
showing little or no decorum,
little or no pomp.
This wasn't the first time we'd had three or four
jorums

too many. For years the heavens had pummeled
us not only with regulation hail
but blow bolts sledged with the comal
tufts of bulrush or cattail.

It seemed marsh elder still made for a blowgun
that raised itself like its own slogan
while "Bring it on"
was the rallying cry
of the thistles now at daggers drawn
that had once seen eye to eye.

New Poems

Hunting With Eagles,
Western Mongolia, 2016

1

Only when an eagle has recovered from her summer moult
and the larch lost its needles
may the hunt begin in earnest. Our breakfast of mutton in mild
broth with broad rice noodles

should tide us over till lunch;
that the eagle herself is working on an empty belly
explains her chirruping and why, given the chance to launch
herself off a ridge, she'll usually fall for the ploy

of a strip of sheep-lung lodged in Agalai's glove
and promptly fly to him. Eagle on arm, Agalai steers his pony
straight up the face of a cliff
while we continue to skirt the base. My 100% yak wool beanie

and 100% yak wool sweater might stand me in better stead
against the wind were there not still snow
on the far peaks. Myself and four other beaters study
the valley floor for a news-

flash from one of the red foxes
that prey on sheep and goats. And that goes directly to the point
of training an eagle in the first place, why Agalai fixes
on her head a little leather bonnet

like a scold's cap, removing it only so her sharp
eye may glimpse,
beyond the sagebrush and other shrubs,
a totality of sorts. As Agalai releases her she climbs

an air current the better to scry
the fox we flush from cover only to watch it scurry
across the scree like a wraith
of itself before almost straightaway going to earth.

2

Maybe it's somewhere near this spot that the drama
of the burial of Genghis Khan
unfolded. The talk last night was all of Clinton and Trump,
the US refusal to allow Bin Laden to become an icon

by burying him in a secret grave, then cutting out the tongues
of the burial party. At the dead center
of my *ger* is a stove that burns 100% yak dung
and dry sticks. Last night I was worried a cinder

might set fire to a wall
hanging woven from some of the finest wool
from some of the finest lambs that ever gamboled
in this vale – hangings the more compelling for being incomplete.

3

That these ornate wall hangings fall short of the raked soil
of the *ger* floor is meant to symbolize our fallings short
right along the sill
of the world. My guide was shrewd

enough to know my horse might have a mind
to be persnickety and had lengthened my stirrups
accordingly to make it easier to dismount.
Even at this remove we could hear the eagle's chirrups

cut short as she was once again bent
upon a fox. Once again we watched it lope
out of view. Once again the bond
endured and the eagle flew to Agalai, paying more than lip

service to the idea that we live from precipice to precipice,
that a hope quickly kindled
may be as quickly quenched. Now we've stopped for lunch I pose
with the eagle on a gauntlet

and persuade myself I belong
to the line of *berkutchi* in a Bronze Age petroglyph
who first held out the hope of a strip of sheep-lung.
Surely a forebear of this eagle would have served the Caliph

of Baghdad? Because of the prowess
as hunters of her lineage,
this is but one of successive chicks Agalai has gone back to prise
from the same ledge-nest. Only when she seems to lunge

at me with a half-hearted yelp
do I sense just how precipitously she might elbow
me out. A primrose cere highlighting her pewter beak,
she grips my arm as if about to let me in on something really big.

Walnuts

1

Bringing to mind the hemispheres of the brain in the brainpan,
these walnut halves are as ripe
for pickling now as in 860, the dye in a Viking girl's underdress
then being derived from walnut husks. I hear you stifle
a yawn when I note that steamed
black walnut is generally held to be inferior to kiln-dried
while the term *à la mode de Caen*
refers specifically to the braising of tripe
in apple cider. I who have been at the mercy of the cider-press
have also been known to trifle
with the affections of a dryad in a sacred grove,
a judge's daughter and a between-maid to Lord Mountbatten
among others from beyond my clan.
It was only as recently as 1824 we first used the term "to snipe."
Walnut was the go-to stock wood for both Brown Bess
and the Lee-Enfield bolt-action, magazine-fed, repeating rifle.
Each has seen service on the shores of Lough Erne
in the hands of both wood-kernes and followers of the First Earl.

2

Our own interpersonal relationships have tended to be so askew
it was only as recently as 1844 we first used the term "scarf"
of the neck-garter. Girding up the loins
for a family feud has often proved the more fecund
line of inquiry. Walnuts are now deemed
good against malignancies of breast and prostate – not only tried
but tried and true. From time to time you
and I have met on a windswept airfield or wharf

where we've seen fit to join
battle without ever having reckoned
on how the Irish law on treasure trove
would change in the light of the Derrynaflan paten
never mind King Sitric being the son-in-law of King Brian Boru
who prevailed over him at Clontarf
or, at the Boyne,
William of Orange's putting paid to his father-in-law, James II.
It was at the Boyne, you recall, that Ahern
gave Paisley the "peace bowl" turned from a local walnut-burl.

Zoological Positivism Blues

Come with me to the petting zoo
Its waist high turnstile gate
Come with me to the petting zoo
We'll prove it's not too late
For them to corner something new
They can humiliate
You know the zoo in Phoenix Park
Began with one wild boar
It's in the zoo in Phoenix Park
We heard the lion roar
And disappointment made its mark
On the thorn forest floor

I guess we'll hire two folding bikes
They rent them by the day
I guess we'll hire two folding bikes
And you'll meet me halfway
Why do orangutans look like
They're wearing bad toupees?
The mealworm and the cricket snacks
The tender foliage
The mealworm and the cricket snacks
They're still stored in a fridge
For when the polar bears start back
Across the old land bridge

You snuggled up to me at dawn
For fear I'd oversleep
You snuggled up to me at dawn
The tickets are dirt cheap
For outings in the carriage drawn

By two Merino sheep
So come with me to the petting zoo
And we'll see how things stand
Come with me to the petting zoo
I'll learn to take commands
I'm sure we'll find something to do
If we've time on our hands

April In New Hope

Ascribe it though we may to the McCormick clan
the technology of the mechanical reaper and hay tedder
had been developed by the Celts
before being lost with Rome. A Cambridge man
might be done for by a "bedder"
but Princeton men kept slaves. In 1849, the Corn Belt

still stretched to the Delaware.
We few, we happy few, are still so newfangled
with our own Henriad
we forget New Hope is where
each generation is doomed to wrangle
the shad roe from the shad

only to pair them once again, fried in bacon fat
and served on a white platter
with capers and lime.
By 1949, Richard Feynman was already plugging away at
the idea of antimatter being matter
that merely goes backwards in time.

Cuttlebone

[instrumental]

Here's to the bitter leaf
On top of the flagpole
Here's to what comes to grief
On a coral shoal
You'll be the last overkill
By the first airborne
You'll be the cornmill
I'll be the corn

Check out the nuclear theater
Where I set the stage
When a private investigator
Asked about your age

You'll be my sole survivor
I'll be your fallout zone
You'll be my pearldiver
I'll be your diving stone
You'll be my pearldiver
I'll be your diving stone

Here's to brisket of beef
Mustard and mayonnaise
Here's to our commander in chief
Out to lunch in the maze
You'll be three bags full
I'll be Samson shorn
You'll be Sitting Bull
At the Little Big Horn

Check out the high pressure
I found so hard to gauge
When you took that refresher
Course on riot and rampage

You'll be my crazy diamond
I'll be your Sierra Leone
You'll be my crime and
I'll be your sentence postponed

[bridge]

Till we've all been sold up the river to sing sing
With nothing to show but our clipped wings
And the Pink Floyd album we thought we'd outgrown
But listen to now on one set of earphones

[instrumental]

Here's to the cherished belief
We must sacrifice our kids
Here's to the data thief
Now living off the grid
You'll be a tinker's dam
I'll be your firstborn
You'll be the luckless ram
Caught up in the thorn

Check out the Bay State hymnal
And my earmarked page
When that cyber criminal
First hacked into your cage

You'll be my Syd Barrett
I'll be your anticyclone
You'll be my red-billed parrot

I'll be your cuttlebone
You'll be my red-billed parrot
I'll be your cuttlebone

[instrumental]

Every Town It Had A Mayor

Again we tumbled through Tombstone
Through Florence and Fort Worth
Dodge city Athens and Athlone
Saint Petersburg and Perth
You were rolling hashish in a blunt
At a time most ladies wore a gown
Every gown had an elastic front
Every last frontier a town

Every town it had a mayor
Every mayor he had a chain
Every chain it had a link
What that link said was try again
Try again try again
That link said try again

Again we pottered through Pottsdam
Through Saigon and Stockholm
Reykjavik and Nottingham
Persepolis and Rome
I was getting ready for a spasm
At a time most tyrants kept a clown
Every clown honoring sarcasm
Every one-ring circus honoring the town

A circus might pitch its tent some night
And leave the townsfolk touched by blight
Just as you touched me in my pain
When you said we should try again
Try again try again

Again we backpacked through Peekskill
Through Carthage and New York
Oxford and Cambridge and Nashville
West Nineveh and Cork
We were eating pasta with red sauce
At a time most bishops wore a crown
Every crown crowned with a fiery cross
Every ferry crossing a town

Every town it had a mayor
Every mayor he had a chain
Every chain it had a link
What that link said was try again
Every chain it had a link
What that link said was try again
Every chain it had a link
What that link said was try again

I Gave The Pope A Rhino

1

I gave the pope a rhino
That had tossed on its horn
The leopard from Inferno
The night our vows were sworn
For being staunch
Doesn't mean you can't launch
An all-out attack
Though it may rush
Through the underbrush
At least it's still on track
I gave the pope a rhino
To show which path is true . . .
Everything that's left
I'll give to you
Everything that's left
I'll give to you

2

I gave the Tsar a sturgeon
From the Caspian Sea
We associate the region
With instability
But doubling the locks
May well replenish stocks
In the longer term
Though its hold
Is slender we're told
At least its grasp is firm

I gave the Tsar a sturgeon
To show what's been renewed . . .
Everything that's left
I'll give to you
Everything that's left
I'll give to you

[bridge]

My bow of burning gold
My scrip of joy immortal diet
A bar of soap I stole
From the Hyannis Port Hyatt
Regency
A fingernail of Charles the Bold
A first edition of Johnny Panic
A first class dinner roll
From the RMS Titanic
Lost at sea
Rembrandt's recipe for raw umber
A bamboo strainer and a sieve
To catch prime numbers
A bootlace tie worn by a Spiv
In E2
A bootleg of the X-pensive Winos
A tortoise we've so far outlived
A spare black rhino
Everything that's left I'll give
To you to you to you to you

3

I gave the prince a diamond
I picked up in the grass
He may yet sieze the moment
Through a pane of glass

We know that to cower
In a crystal tower
Makes it hard to find a match
Though he's barely touched
The surface as such
At least that surface is scratched
I gave the prince a diamond
To show how to cut through ...
Everything that's left
I'll give to you
Everything that's left
I'll give to you

Likely To Go Unnoticed

Amid acres of rapeseed, a streak of ragwort
may yet shine
as an off-the-record
remark becomes the party line,

as a dray in saddle-pad and blinders
doing shit work
on the streets outsplendors
the Byerley Turk,

as a yellow truck that's missed its exit
on a roundabout (perhaps because of a dearth
of signage?), repeats one word –

HORSES – at which it has itself but guessed.
The roundabout's named after Maria Edgeworth
of Edgeworthstown, County Longford.

Lonesome George

[Musical intro based on rhythm of chorus]

Verse 1

They used to say
You ought to stay
Down on the farm
Where the grass is green
They used to say
You should make hay
Till you lose an arm
To a mowing machine
Now they say
That you can fly
Twice a day
From Dublin to Dubai

[chorus]

Let's go back to living on the edge
Let's go back to how it used to be
Let's go back to living on the edge
I want you to stay with staying with me

Verse 2

They used to say
You ought to stay
Within the sound of church bells
Or the factory horn
They used to say
You should wait for a ray

To break through to your cell
One December morn
Now they say
That you can fly
Twice a day
From Galway

[segue into bridge]

To the Galapagos and gallop there
Through Vulcan's Forge
Maybe even let down your hair
With a tortoise called Lonesome George

[instrumental]

Verse 3

They used to say
You ought to stay
With your seed and breed
On a moonlit hill
They used to say
Six feet of clay
Is all you need
To be promised in a will
Now they say
That you can fly
Twice a day
From Shannon to Shanghai

[chorus]

Let's go back to living by our pledge
Let's go back to how it used to be
Let's go back to living by our pledge
I want you to stay with staying with me

Afterword

Proofing a book is so different from reading a book (count the repetitions of 'm' in 'emmmmmmmmmmmmmmphasize!'), trusting in the text. To proof is not to trust the text. Somehow, I think this distrust suits interphasing with Muldoon's language and voice shifts and 'plays', and in doing so certain notions recur to me that I'd like to state as a starting point for signing off, for 'closure' in a Muldoon poem always seems the rounding-out of a set of possibilities in order to suggest another set of possibilities.

Aside from *Madoc*, which I am considering in the context of a longer future critical work, and whose counter-indicative voicings are an undoing of the blitheness of incipient and accruing Romantic gathering of all to the poetic conversation, I am overwhelmed by the ongoing concern in Muldoon's poetry from the late 1960s through to the end of the second decade of the twenty-first century, with the persistently active dislocations of colonialism, and the irony of colonialisms occurring within colonialisms: the framework of English language Muldoon uses is constantly being eroded and corroded out of a necessity of refusing to let it be stable, have its way over other languages it looks to absorb, to synthesise, and to meld into its own shape. The imagination is never enough, but without it, we are bereft. The contradictions (and anachronisms) of an ongoing search for liberty that deprives others of their liberty are subtext to so much activity in Muldoon word*ploys*.

This applies to all languages of colonisation, and how what is not available to them in a material sense — even with spiritual matters — then *demands* to be made empirical (mapped, defined, quantified) — and Muldoon's irony is at its sharpest in such occlusions. In *Madoc*, we read a *citing* of 'Ordway' sublimated via 'Schelling': 'as though they had an Impediment in their Speech', to refer to the real and conceptual/literary violation of other peoples' integrities. For me, this emphasis of Muldoon's on the delusions of the 'Romantic imagination', the consequences of 'pleasure dome' envisioning, translates into the realtime of historic-adventurism, the assaults and thefts, the colonial economics and survivalism, parsed into fragmented 'accounts' and 'encounters', via the failure of most if not all 'epics' (or faux-epics) to account for the depth and complexities of consequence.

'Sentiment' is never a way out or through, ironically or otherwise, and coming from a particular spatiality of 'The Troubles' — consider 'Flags and Emblems' — (and 'small town' and 'rurality' — on the farm, born in County Armagh and growing up near the small town of Moy, on the boundary of County Armagh and County Tyrone, The Moy being on the Tyrone side of the River Blackwater — and tracing other tensions and pressures within this) and migrating to America, and sharing belongings, Muldoon knows the contradiction, though he is aware it cannot be applied as template because every occupation and dispossession is different, and no creative work for an audience of privilege can counter it, whatever its drives.

It became so clear to me as I proofed and thought over what I'd written about this selection of poems, how much Muldoon deplores, cajoles and even mocks, while trying to generate a language of investigation and scrutiny of such oppressions. At the essence of these poems — as they are inverting syntax, moving across different tonal registers in a short space of a single poem, juxtaposing then dividing meaning — is the integrity of trying to *test* the paradoxes through language being freed of its official legitimised registers of 'communication'.

Even in his 'chatty' voice-orientated poems, seeming certainties are always disrupted, with self-doubt and even self-mockery given gentle-to-intense sway, depending. I think of his animal poems that often deal with a human usage (eating, killing/trophies), yet indicate some kind of animal refusal, denial or even comeback — these are poems of internal struggle almost 'joked' about in public. The serious, in Muldoon, is so serious, it has to be performed, enacted, played out. Witness the fate of the elephant Topsy (yes, I come back to Topsy, haunted), the 'inventiveness' of Thomas

Edison (and his 6000 volts), and tyranny (KGB etc.) in general, in the defamiliarising sequence, 'Plan B' (quick lines can stretch, short rhymes pull us up, repetitions entrap us).

Is this a kind of détournement? Maybe, but it's also something to do with dislocations of migration, colonisation, settlement, intrusion, welcome, and a restive internalising of external tensions. Roused by the storyline, and its tangents, I often find myself thinking of the pace of Byron's *Don Juan*, though, again, slant, and with somewhat different ironies. And confronted by some of the 'speakers' and/or 'subjects' (take those sonnetised in 'Maggot') of the poems, as often as not, revulsion banters with compulsion. Always the phrase, the anecdote, the snippet of info, the gleaning from diverse savoury and unsavoury sources, the refrain, the cascade, the source of the compulsiveness.

Whether read in Belfast, Dublin or New York, or some other town or city of the world, one has the feeling that a Muldoon poem, however locale-specific, is always travelling, gathering and collating experience, knowledge and observations. The pastoral is so place-specific, but Muldoon gives it pace and movement. His persistent undoing of, yet also rapture at literary pastoral finds its most concentrated expression in the poems of *Hay* (1998), especially in the tour de force of 'The Mud Room'. We flow and twist our way through 'land' and cultural associations, meldings and juxtapositions; we follow the fate of the 'she-goat' and the singers through this eclogue, this pastoral love poem of not only cultural bridging but almost joyous synthesis. We follow religion and secularism, follow 'tradition' via modernity; the field is opened up and we experience Passover/Seder, we encounter faith in being, in love, in welcome, in a rolling celebration that also plays the ironies of the quotidian, of getting through... as we participate vicariously as readers in the breaking of unleavened bread. Throughout the *Hay* poems (and the title poem 'Hay' not being included here is more about mode than what it has to say — it is the motif poem of its own book), the tropes and motifs of the pastoral are played out, toyed with, indulged, rejected, and rewritten. And we see that in the metonymic plays of 'The Symposium' that bind *and* undo, that connect and disconnect, drawing the associative nature of Muldoon's poetics into a particular focus (one of many); they remind me of spells, charms and prayers, as well as jokes and aphorisms turning on themselves, while inter-related. And even rock music in its many manifestations encounters origins with varying degrees of certainty and dismissal, suspicion and embrace, in poems of ironic ebullience such as 'Cream: *Disraeli Gears*' — 'Georgiks and Bukoliks'.

Muldoon often turns to art and artists, to other creative texts or their creators, possibly in an attempt to refocalise his poetics, to add more doubt to his ongoing doubt: the more visceral the language, the more febrile the ideas and ethical search behind it. When I finish, it's the great elegy to artist Mary Farl Powers I think over, that puts all Muldoon's language-shifts into a kind of perspective: of compassion, of sharing, of scrutiny with wit and generosity of spirit, of Beckett's *Waiting for Godot*. His telling — his singing (often dancing, certainly performing) — the story of a friendship, an admiration, and it occurs to me that so much of his work is story-telling at slant, a case of dislocated quests.

John Kinsella, August 2020